Contents

How to use this book

Welcome!

Revise for GCSE Citizenship Studies for AQA has been written to help you revise successfully for your Citizenship Studies examination.

Being a citizen

For yourself, in your relationships with others, as a member of society and as a global citizen, you need to:

- have good self-esteem
- take responsibility for your own actions
- work co-operatively with others
- respect the law and justice
- promote equality of opportunity
- uphold a person's human rights.

As a citizen, you should reflect on local, national and global issues and formulate your own opinions. You should remember that your opinion should be based on fact and you should provide evidence to support your view. Your opinion should be expressed clearly without being offensive to others and it should reflect your feelings about the issues you have studied.

Your course

The GCSE Short Course in Citizenship Studies has three main topics:

- **Topic 1**   School, work and the local community
- **Topic 2**   National and European citizenship
- **Topic 3**   Global citizenship.

In addition, the course has three themes:

- **Theme 1**   Rights and responsibilities
- **Theme 2**   Decision-making, power and authority
- **Theme 3**   Participation in citizenship activities.

The examination paper will expect you to show knowledge and understanding of the topics and the themes.

What you should know

Each chapter begins with the key points that you need to know in each area of study.

Every page is packed with margin notes to help highlight what you need to know.

Margin Notes

Key words

Important words and terms are in bold print throughout the book. You need to make sure that you know what these words and terms mean. Check them in the textbook, the glossary or a dictionary.

did you know?

These short pieces of information are additions to your knowledge and can be used as examples in examination answers.

Hints and tips

These are brief notes to help you with your revision or examination technique.

exam watch

These brief notes aim to help you with examination answers and techniques.

The exam paper

As you know, the exam paper will be in the form of a booklet containing the questions and spaces for your answers. You MUST answer all the questions in Sections A, B and C and one of the three questions in Section D. Each section of the paper is worth a total of 30 marks.

Section A questions require short factual answers. These questions will be similar to those at the end of each chapter (*see also* pages 85–88).

Section B will give a piece of written information for you to read and answer questions on. For the answers use the information given in the text and your own knowledge. Give facts, examples and opinions as appropriate (for examples of Section B questions for each chapter, *see* pages 62–69).

Section C will have questions about the coursework or any other citizenship activity you may have taken part in (*see* pages 70–71). Read the question carefully before answering.

Section D, there is a choice here: you MUST answer one of the three questions which will be on the different themes that run throughout the course (*see* pages 72–84).

Read ALL the questions. THEN choose the one you know most about to answer. There will be some points to help you structure your answer. You should include some *facts*, *examples* and *evidence* to show how you have formed any opinions you give.

Examples of the types of questions in Sections B and D and how you would be expected to answer them are separate chapters in this book. There is also a shorter chapter on Section C.

Some general hints on revision

- Start your revision about two months before the examination.
- Organize your revision so that you read a certain number of pages each week.
- Work through each of the sections carefully and methodically.
- Find *evidence* and *examples* to support each issue.
- Take regular short breaks: you could have a drink/snack, phone a friend or listen to some music every 45mins–1hour.
- Use the checklist for revision at the end of each chapter to help you organize your revision timetable.
- Finally, revise again the issues you don't know.

We hope you find this book useful in achieving the success you deserve.

Action Point Ⓐ

Action Points ask you to do something. They are there to help you reflect as you re-read and re-learn citizenship issues. Action Points are designed to help you prepare to answer the examination questions in the book.

Key ideas

These are short descriptions of important ideas that will help you relate the themes to the topics.

look back

These short guidelines tell you where to find more detailed information in the revision book or the textbook. They encourage you to look for detailed information if you are unsure of the issues being discussed.

School, work and the local community

1 School

What you need to know

- What are basic human rights and how they were established
- What is meant by legal and moral rights and responsibilities
- What are power and authority and how people in school have different types of power and authority
- The school community and the local community and how they interrelate
- Equal opportunities — what it means and how it may be promoted in school
- Discrimination, racism, racial prejudice and stereotyping, what these terms mean and how they can be avoided
- The laws affecting equal opportunities and race relations, and organizations working in these areas

Human rights

The Council of Europe (consisting of 39 countries) was set up after World War II and produced the European Convention on Human Rights (ECHR). The purpose was to guarantee the citizens of all the countries that ratified the convention 16 basic human rights.

The European Court of Human Rights sits in Strasbourg and anyone who believes that their human rights have been violated by a government may take their case to this court. The court makes a judgement which is then carried out by the Committee of Ministers.

The UK was one of the original members of the Council of Europe who ratified the Convention, but it was not until 1998 that there was human rights legislation here. The Human Rights Act was passed in 1998. The full force of this act came into being in October 2000.

The effects of the act are as follows:
- The ECHR is now part of UK law.
- UK citizens can take a disputed human rights case to a UK court.
- Courts here and in Europe can make judgements on human rights issues.
- These rights can only be changed by parliament.

exam watch

Use examples from your own experience to back up a point where you can. Use the textbook and the work you have done throughout the course for reference.

exam watch

You should be able to explain at least six of the basic human rights with examples.

Hints and tips

You need to be able to write about the effects of the Human Rights Act.

Legal and moral rights and responsibilities

Definitions: you need to know these and be able to write about them in an exam – remember to give examples if you are asked to.

A right is something we are all entitled to (these are sometimes referred to as freedoms or entitlements).

A responsibility is something that we are expected to do.

Rights and responsibilities may be either legal or moral.

A legal right or **responsibility** is what we can do or what we are responsible for according to the law.

A moral right or **responsibility** is what we are expected to do.

These expectations are determined by the society we live in. They are known as the values of our society – what is deemed to be good and worthwhile. Different cultures have different values and expectations, therefore they will have different moral rights and responsibilities.

Children are some of the most vulnerable people in society and their rights are covered by the Children Act of 1989. This act has the well-being of children at its core. The opinions of children must be taken into account in a variety of situations by law.

look back

See pages 12–14 of the textbook.

	Rights	Responsibilities
Pupils	A safe place to learn	To obey the school rules
Parents	To decide which religion children are brought up in	To ensure children attend school
Teachers	To expect pupils to behave reasonably	To mark and assess pupils' work

Action Point

Draw up a table to show the rights and responsibilities of children, parents and teachers. Use the chart on the left as a guide. One example has been included, you should be able to think of at least three others for each heading. *Learn the chart.*

Power and authority in school

Definitions you should learn:

Power is the ability to influence or to rule. This may be one person or a group of people.

Authority is a form of power which is accepted as a legal right to command or rule.

Coercion is rule by force.

look back

See pages 15–17 of the textbook.

The Local Education Authority allocates an amount of money – the school budget – to the school governors and head teacher, who are responsible for managing how this money is spent. This is known as economic power.

The school community

pupils   school governors   heads of year/house
non-teaching staff   senior teachers   parents
heads of faculty   teachers   technicians
educational welfare officers   learning mentors

All the people listed above have a different role in a school, some will have more than one. They will all have specific responsibilities and duties they are expected to carry out.

Most of the people mentioned will work in the school and make up the **school community**, sharing the same values and following the same set of 'rules'.

You probably discussed school rules during the course – why they are important, who makes the rules, who enforces the rules, what happens if the rules are broken, what would happen if there were no rules, how rules are changed, etc.

You will have been given many opportunities to be a valued member of your school community, by taking responsibility for a task, helping others, being a member of a sports team, after-school club, school choir, drama group, etc. This means taking some responsibility and being reliable. These are important attributes of a responsible citizen, can you explain why?

Many schools have a school council which encourages pupils to participate in democratic elections and enables those elected to represent the views of others in discussions which may result in some changes being made.

The local community

A **community** is made up of all the people who live in an area, as well as the facilities and services that exist in that location.

Action Point

Many people have power and authority in schools. List as many different people and groups as you can think of that exist within your school. Describe what type of power they have or how they exercise their authority. Use the list on the left to help you.

Action Point

Write a paragraph about 'what makes your school a community'.

See pages 18–22 of the textbook.

Action Point

Write a paragraph about 'how democratic your school is' giving clear reasons and examples.

A school is an important part of any community. Many schools play a great part in their community, by inviting others into school for concerts, pantomimes, plays, etc. Some schools provide facilities and courses for people of all ages, encouraging a greater understanding between people of different ages and cultures, creating a sense of identity and belonging to a wider community.

Remember that the local council is responsible for providing services such as schools, parks, libraries, police, fire brigade, street lighting, social services. Other services we take for granted are healthcare by doctors, health visitors and dentists. Facilities such as leisure centres, sports/health club/gym, cinema, youth clubs, play groups, etc may be found in a community, depending on its size. Rural communities (those in country areas) do not always have as many services and facilities as those in urban areas (towns and cities).

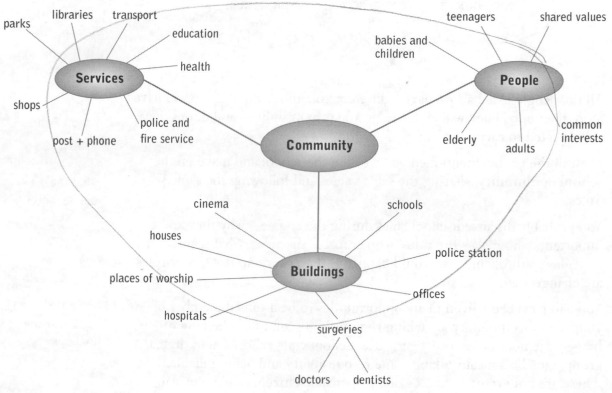

A community ideas web

Equal opportunities

Equal opportunities means that no one should be **discriminated** against (treated differently) because of their gender, race, religion, age, or disability. Everyone should have an equal opportunity based on their ability, there should be fair treatment for everyone. No one should be discriminated against because they are different in some way.

Girls and boys should be treated in exactly the same way; for example, there should be no differences in the way good behaviour is rewarded or inappropriate behaviour is dealt with.

In schools there are many ways in which equal opportunities are promoted:
- all areas of the school should be welcoming to both boys and girls
- the same access is given to all subjects in the curriculum
- the same advice, guidance and opportunities in making career choices
- displays around school, posters, visual aids in classrooms, textbooks
- discussions encouraging positive attitudes towards equality of opportunity
- special activities; for example, equal opportunities days, multicultural day/evening, inviting people from different cultures or religions to talk to groups in school
- visits arranged to different places within the community.

The Equal Opportunities Commission (EOC) was established under the Sex Discrimination Act of 1975. It is an independent public body which works to eliminate sex discrimination in all its forms. The Commission is funded through the Women and Equality Unit at the Department of Trade and Industry and is responsible to the Equality Minister.

The Commission campaigns for:
- equal pay for equal work for men and women
- the promotion of equal opportunities
- the removal of stereotypes.

It also provides advice and information to companies and individuals.

More can be found by visiting www.heinemann.co.uk/hotlinks and inputting express code **8265P**.

Racism

Racism is a belief that people of a particular race are inferior or superior.

Racial prejudice is the forming of an opinion or judgement about a race or ethnic group without real knowledge of that race or group.

Racial discrimination is when a person is treated less favourably than others because of their race.

Stereotyping is the ideas we have about a certain type of person or group through the attitudes we have learned or acquired, this is not based on knowledge of a person or group.

The Race Relations Act

The Commission for Racial Equality (CRE) was set up by the Race Relations Act of 1976. The CRE receives a grant from the government but carries out its work independently.

Hints and tips

Make sure you know about the ways in which equal opportunities are promoted in schools.

exam watch

Always learn what every abbreviation stands for. They are likely questions in Section A of the exam paper.

The Commission for Racial Equality has three functions:

- to try to eliminate racial discrimination and promote equality of opportunity
- to encourage good relations between people from different backgrounds
- to monitor the way the Race Relations Act is working and recommend improvements.

Rights under the Race Relations Act

It is against the law:

- for a person to be treated less favourably than others because of their race, colour, nationality or ethnicity
- to print and distribute material that is likely to cause racial hatred
- to publish material in the media that is racially offensive
- to use adverts which are racially offensive.

The Race Relations Act was amended in 2000 and this imposes responsibilities on public authorities to promote racial equality in education, training, jobs, housing and services.

The Institute of Race Relations is another independent body which researches and analyses information about racial discrimination and racial justice in the UK and Europe.

Try these short questions

Questions like the ones below will appear in Section A of the exam paper. They require short, factual answers and are worth two marks for each question. Answers to these questions can be found on page 85.

1 List four basic human rights.
2 Explain the term 'a legal right' and give an example.
3 What is a moral responsibility? Give an example.
4 List two effects of the Human Rights Act of 1998.
5 Define the terms 'power' and 'coercion'.
6 What is the difference between a rural and urban community?
7 Explain the term 'equality of opportunity'.
8 What does 'EOC' stand for?
9 How and when was the Commission for Racial Equality set up?
10 What is racial discrimination?

Action Point Ⓐ

Test yourself by answering the questions and then looking up the answers. Be honest with yourself – find out what you know and what you still need to learn!

Checklist for revision

	Know and understand	Need more revision	Do not know
Basic human rights and how they were established	☐	☐	☐
Definitions of legal and moral rights and responsibilities	☐	☐	☐
Power and authority	☐	☐	☐
The school community and the local community	☐	☐	☐
Equal opportunities – what it means and how it is promoted	☐	☐	☐
Discrimination, racism, prejudice and stereotyping	☐	☐	☐
Laws affecting equal opportunities and race relations, and related organizations	☐	☐	☐

exam watch

Make a revision map for your bedroom wall. Stick up news headlines by topic. Have fun with it.

2 Work

What you need to know

- The rights and responsibilities of employers and employees
- Major acts of parliament concerned with employment
- Health and safety at work
- Types of business ownership
- Industry sectors – what they are and examples of each type
- The national and local economy
- Banks and business finance
- Personal finance

Action Point Ⓐ

Produce a chart to show a comparison between responsibilities of an employer and an employee.

See page 30 of the textbook.

The rights and responsibilities of employers and employees

Both employers and employees have legal and moral rights and responsibilities towards each other. The legal responsibilities are defined in a number of Acts of Parliament which cover all aspects of employment, from recruitment to redundancy, across all types of business and sectors of production.

Contracts of employment

Employers must supply every employee with a **contract of employment**. This is a written document stating the terms and conditions of employment and must include:

- name of employer and employee
- job title
- place(s) of work
- date of starting employment
- working hours
- rate of pay
- how payment will be made
- holiday entitlement
- sick pay entitlement
- pension schemes, if any
- details of complaints and disciplinary procedures
- grievance procedures
- conditions for terminating employment for both parties.

Major acts of parliament concerned with employment

The Employment Rights Act 1996 is the main act which covers employment law. The emphasis of this act is that everyone, regardless of race, gender, age or disability has equal rights and opportunities for recruitment, pay and promotion.

Three other important acts deal with all aspects of discrimination in recruitment and working practices, they are: The Sex Discrimination Act 1975; The Race Relations Act 1976; and The Disability Discrimination Act 1995. Other acts dealing with employment are:

- **The National Minimum Wage Act 1998** states the minimum wage that must be paid to employees according to their age.
- **The EU Working Time Directive 1998** brought in the limit of 48 hours for a working week.
- **The Workplace Regulations 1992** deals with EU rules, including the safe use of computers.
- **The Employment Protection Act 1978** is concerned with redundancy, unfair dismissal and tribunals.

Health and safety at work

The Health and Safety Commission (HSC) has overall responsibility for setting policy on health and safety matters. The Health and Safety Executive (HSE) ensures that employers take full responsibility for their employees; that employees look after their own safety and that no harm is done to members of the public through work-related activities.

The Factories Act 1961 and **The Health and Safety Act 1974** are the major acts which deal with **health and safety at work**. The Health and Safety Act 1974 made employers and employees responsible for working together to ensure safe and healthy working practices. Employers must provide training for the job and employees must raise concerns about health and safety issues if they think a situation or work practice is dangerous or unhealthy. The HSE enforces the law and gives advice and guidance to individuals and companies about how the requirements of the law may be met.

Workers wearing hard hats on a building site

Types of business ownership

The main types of ownership are:

- **A sole trader** – one person owns and runs a business, has total control, provides the **finance**, takes the risks and keeps the profits.

- **A partnership** – from 2 to 20 people agree to run a company. The partners provide the finance and make all the decisions, sharing risks, responsibilities and profit.

- **A public limited company (plc)** – is run by a board of directors. The shareholders provide the finance by buying the shares on the stock exchange. An annual general meeting must be held for the shareholders.

- **A private limited company (Ltd)** – is a company owned by a small number of shareholders. The shares are not traded on the stock exchange and may only be bought by the people who started the company.

- **A franchise** – is when a person (the franchisee) buys a franchise from a successful well known company to run a similar company along specific lines. The franchisee has to pay the franchisor a percentage of the annual profits.

- **A co-operative** – is where all the workers buy shares in the business, they are involved in all financial matters and decision making, and share the profits.

Examples of different types of businesses

Industry sectors

All production for **industry** is divided into one of four different sectors.

- The **primary** sector extracts raw materials and natural resources from the ground or the sea. It includes farming, fishing, mining and quarrying.
- The **secondary** sector uses the raw materials gathered or grown by the primary sector to make something and a completed product.
- The **tertiary** sector is the service sector. Services may be provided to industry or **consumers**. This sector includes services such as police, fire, education and health.
- The **quaternary** sector is also a service sector. It has been developed through the use of technology and involves telecommunications and the Internet in such facilities as call centres, on-line shopping and banking services.

Action Point Ⓐ

Make a list of some companies you know, then decide which industry sector they operate in and what type of ownership they have. Try to include some national and local businesses.

The national and local economy

The **economy** is the way in which goods, services and finances are provided and managed.

Every country has its own way of organizing and managing its national economy. Economists define four types of economy:

- **Subsistence economy** – seen in Less Economically Developed Countries (LEDCs) – where people grow their own food and build their own houses from natural resources. There is very little trade or production of goods and services.
- **Market economy** – where the demand for goods and services drives the economy. Demand is supplied by businesses, mostly in private ownership, or by multinational companies. This type of economy is seen in the More Economically Developed Countries (MEDCs).
- **Planned economy** – the state owns most of the businesses and decides what will be produced. Consumers have little influence over the types of goods and services.
- **Mixed economy** – a combination of a market and planned economy, where most businesses are motivated by profit and supply consumer demand for goods and services. Some businesses and services are owned and run by the government; for example, the National Health Service in Britain. This type of economy is seen in many MEDCs.

exam watch

Can you name countries where each type of economy exists?

The national economy

The UK has a mixed economy. There are many businesses and multinational companies producing a wide variety of goods and services to satisfy consumer demand.

A strong economy is important to create wealth and prosperity for the citizens of a country. This is generated by trading with other countries – selling manufactured products to others (exports) and buying goods from other countries (imports). The balance of payments is the difference between the cost of imports and exports. If a country exports more goods than it imports, it is said to have a positive balance of payments and a strong economy, because the businesses are growing and expanding and employing more people. If the cost of imports is more than the cost of exports, there is said to be a negative balance of payments and the economy will be weak and unemployment will increase.

It has been seen that as the more traditional industries of coal mining, ship building and steel production have declined, other new industries have grown up to take their place, such as the service, information technology, leisure and fast food industries.

In recent years the advances in information technology and the use of computers has had a huge influence on business and trade. The way companies operate, trade and advertise has been revolutionized – now most organizations rely on computers and Internet technology. This has been a major growth area and has generated wealth for many companies, regions and countries.

The local economy

This is based on the manufacturing and service industries that operate within an area or region of the country. In some regions the traditional industries, such as coal mining, ship building and steel production, have disappeared and new service industries have taken their place.

In some regions where there has been a decline in manufacturing, it is possible for companies to obtain grants from the government or the EU to set up new businesses to create employment and prosperity for local people. These areas are known as Development Areas or Enterprise Zones.

Banks and businesses

Businesses use financial services in different ways, from using business accounts for payments to be made and banking monies paid to them, to arranging overdrafts, mortgages and loans. Most banks offer services for small businesses helping with advice and drawing up business plans, arranging insurance services, providing telephone or on-line banking.

Companies use financial services in other ways, such as using credit controls so that money owed to them is paid promptly to ensure the company has sufficient funds to cover its outgoings. Some companies may decide to arrange a leasing agreement for expensive equipment or machinery which is needed constantly, so that the outlay is not as great.

Action Point

Name the main employers in your area. What would be the effect on the local economy if one of the major employers ceased trading?

Hire purchase is another form of finance often used to purchase equipment. When all the payments have been made at the end of the agreed term the company will own the equipment.

A company may decide to raise money by being floated on the stock exchange, so shares may be bought and sold by the public. Loans or grants from the government or the EU may be available to set up new businesses in some areas. There are always criteria that have to be satisfied but this type of finance is always worth investigating.

Personal finance

There are different types of accounts offered by banks and building societies and it is important to open the right account to suit your needs. A current account is the most common type of account. You usually need to be 18 years or over to open this type of account. Money may be paid directly into this account, for example by an employer, and you can write cheques to pay for goods or obtain cash by cashing a cheque or using a cash card and PIN (Personal Identification Number) at an ATM (Automatic Teller Machine).

Banks also offer credit cards. These need to be used very carefully because it is extremely easy to build up debts quickly, and the interest rates on the money borrowed are high, unless the balance is paid off (cleared) at the end of each month. The same facts apply to store charge cards. Be careful.

There are a number of options for savings accounts and the best one for you depends on how you want to save and how quickly you may want access to your money. Some types of account will allow you to withdraw a limited amount on demand (without any notice) without losing any interest.

Usually the amount of interest the account earns increases with the length of notice required for withdrawal. For example a 90-day account will accrue more interest than a 30-day account. All types of accounts that pay interest are liable for **tax**.

Key ideas

Remember that interest is the amount of money the account gains over a period of time and is expressed as a percentage.

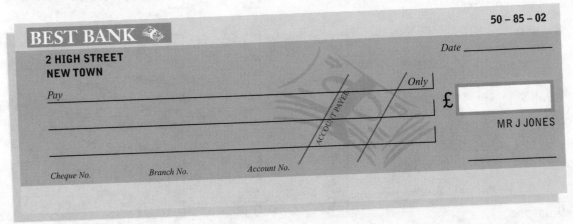

A blank cheque

An ISA is an Individual Savings Account. You do not have to pay any tax on the interest earned in an ISA but there is a limit to the amount of money you can invest in this type of account in any one tax year. There are different types of ISA and it is worth investigating these types of saving accounts.

Try these short questions

Questions like the ones below will appear in Section A of the exam paper. They require short, factual answers and are worth two marks for each question. Answers to these questions can be found on page 85.

1 Give two rights of an employee.
2 What did the Employment Rights Act 1996 emphasize?
3 What is the major Act of Parliament that deals with health and safety at work?
4 Who is responsible for health and safety at work?
5 Name two types of business ownership.
6 Define the secondary sector of industry.
7 Name two multinational companies.
8 What is a mixed economy?
9 Name two traditional industries that have declined in recent years.
10 How old must you be to open a current account with a bank?

Action Point (A)

Test yourself by answering the questions and then looking up the answers. Be honest with yourself – find out what you know and what you still need to learn!

Checklist for revision

	Know and understand	Need more revision	Do not know
Rights and responsibilities of employers and employees	☐	☐	☐
Major acts of parliament concerned with employment	☐	☐	☐
Health and safety at work	☐	☐	☐
The national and local economy	☐	☐	☐
Types of business ownership	☐	☐	☐
Industry sectors – definitions and examples	☐	☐	☐
Banks, business finance and grants	☐	☐	☐
Personal finance	☐	☐	☐

Some people find rewriting and reorganising their class notes helps them remember better!

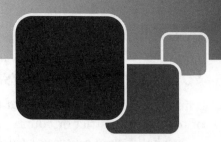

3 The local community

What you need to know

- Factors affecting community life – ethnic identity, religion and culture
- Local government systems
- Financing local services
- Devolution and regional government
- Voting systems
- How individuals can bring about change – political parties, voluntary organizations, pressure groups, focus groups, trade unions
- Protests

Factors affecting community life

Ethnic identity refers to a particular way of life or culture (language, lifestyle and customs) of a group within a society. Within our multi-racial society we are learning and understanding more and more about diverse cultures. When people accept the differences and are tolerant of them, then community life is enriched and harmonious. When people are intolerant, or a group feels discriminated against, then problems arise and trouble can break out.

Religion is a term which means a system of belief in a particular faith, set of values, practices, rites and worship – often of a supernatural power or being. Members of a religious group will hold the same belief and conform to the same set of values. They will support each other through difficulties, creating a sense of belonging and social cohesion. Religions also provide a means of social control because a well-defined code of behaviour is expected. Places of worship can provide points of contact within a community because many offer a range of activities: play groups, youth clubs, luncheon clubs, etc. which are open to all members of the community.

Culture is the shared language, behaviours, customs, traditions and values of a society. The culture patterns of a society are learned during childhood through a process known as socialization. The values of a culture refer to things that people believe are important and worthwhile. Values will change over time within the same society, and some small groups within a society may have slightly different values from the wider culture that they belong to; for example, teenage culture. Identify some differences shown in teenage or youth culture.

Action Point Ⓐ

Learn one or two examples where problems have occurred, either national or local, to use as evidence in an exam question.

See pages 45 and 46 of text book.

Local government systems

There are normally two tiers of **local government**. The first tier consists of town, city, district or county councils and unitary authorities that meet in city halls, civic centres or shire halls. The councillors are elected for a term of four years. Councils are responsible for:

- council housing
- police and fire services
- roads
- leisure, recreation and sports
- education
- pavements and street lighting
- libraries and arts
- social services.

The second tier of local government is the parish council. These cover a much smaller area or parish. Parish councillors are elected for a maximum of four years and are responsible for local services such as village halls, playing fields and rights of way.

New constitution for local authorities

In 2000 the government decided it was time to set up a new constitution for local government. There were three options for the new structure:

- a leader with a cabinet of councillors
- a directly elected mayor with a cabinet of councillors
- a directly elected mayor with a council manager.

All local authorities consulted people, organizations and businesses in their area and in some places a referendum was held and people on the Register of Electors voted for their preference.

Financing local services

Councils are funded from two sources – the local council tax and money given to them by the national government raised in taxes. Special developments may also have finance from central government; for example, meeting the costs of national pay awards.

The local council decides what it wants to spend money on, in line with its policies on such things as education, social services, housing, libraries and arts, sport and recreational facilities, etc. All council services affect the quality of daily life for the residents, so electing your representative – your councillor – is very important. Read information sent out by all the people standing in local elections and decide who you would vote for and why. **Voting** in local elections is one way of making your voice heard, another is to meet your local councillor at a 'surgery' and express your views.

Local councillors will listen to people's opinions and will often pursue matters for individuals, or become involved with local campaigns; for example, school closures or new roads.

exam watch

Make sure you know:
- which structure your local council operates under and how it was chosen
- where your council meets
- which political party is in power on your council
- how your councillors are elected.

Devolution – regional government in the UK

Devolution is the transfer of power to a lower level, especially from central government to local or national administrations; for example, the devolution of power from Westminster to the Scottish Parliament, Welsh Assembly and the Northern Ireland Assembly. There have been proposals for devolution of power to regional assemblies but this has not been decided upon yet.

You need to know these facts about the existing devolved powers:

Action Point (A)

Discuss your views on regional assemblies and an English parliament to look after issues relating to England.

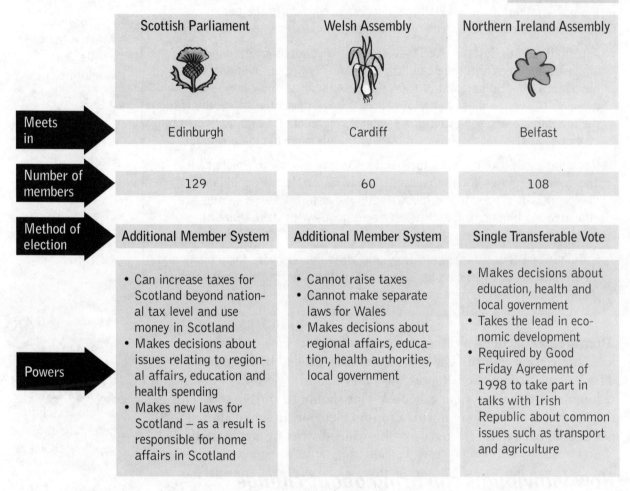

	Scottish Parliament	Welsh Assembly	Northern Ireland Assembly
Meets in	Edinburgh	Cardiff	Belfast
Number of members	129	60	108
Method of election	Additional Member System	Additional Member System	Single Transferable Vote
Powers	• Can increase taxes for Scotland beyond national tax level and use money in Scotland • Makes decisions about issues relating to regional affairs, education and health spending • Makes new laws for Scotland – as a result is responsible for home affairs in Scotland	• Cannot raise taxes • Cannot make separate laws for Wales • Makes decisions about regional affairs, education, health authorities, local government	• Makes decisions about education, health and local government • Takes the lead in economic development • Required by Good Friday Agreement of 1998 to take part in talks with Irish Republic about common issues such as transport and agriculture

The facts about the Scottish Parliament, Welsh and Northern Ireland Assemblies.

Voting systems

This is quite a complex area, you need to understand the different systems and know which systems are used to elect people for the devolved powers and local, national and European elections. You need to be able to state your opinion on the different electoral systems and decide which you think is the fairest and why. You should also be aware of how councils are encouraging more people to vote in elections, such as postal voting and use of the Internet.

Single Transferable Vote – used to elect members of local, regional and European government in Northern Ireland. The number of constituencies is reduced so that each constituency has a greater number of MPs. Voters are required to select candidates in order of preference by placing numbers in descending order against names. The amount of votes a candidate requires to win the seat is determined by the size of the seat. Surplus votes are transferred to other candidates.

Additional Member System – used for elections to the Scottish Parliament and the Welsh Assembly. Half the members are elected using the first past the post system. The other half are selected according to the percentage of votes cast for each party from a list of party nominees in priority order.

Alternative Vote System (AVS) – elects one MP. Voters place numbers against the names of all the candidates in priority order. Candidates must have more than 50 per cent of the votes cast to win. If no candidate achieves this, an exhaustive ballot is held. This removes the candidate with the lowest vote and then counts the voters' second choice and adds it to the other candidates' totals. This continues until only one candidate remains.

Regional List System – used for elections to the European Parliament. The system requires voters to select a party rather than a candidate. The country is divided into regions electing several MPs. The parties are allocated the number of seats which corresponds with their share of the vote.

National List System – used in Italy and Israel. Voters vote for a party and the proportion of votes cast for each party determines the proportion of seats the party will have in government.

Action Point (A)

Think through a possible response to the question 'The present system of first past the post does not represent the wishes of the electorate'. Make a list of points you would include and be able to justify your opinion.

After the 1997 general election the government set up a commission to look at electoral reform. The commission was headed by Lord Jenkins. The Jenkins Commission Report was published in 1998 and recommended that a system called AV plus should be introduced. This is the Alternative Vote System with a top-up element. It would allow 15–20 per cent of MPs to be elected on a city-wide, district or county basis.

Key ideas

A referendum is a vote about a single issue to determine the people's choice.

How individuals can bring about change

Study the definitions below and develop your knowledge about political parties, voluntary organizations, pressure groups, focus groups, trade unions, lobbyists and protests. You should have studied some recent issues involving some of these and have developed your own opinions. You will need to justify these (always use examples to support evidence you are presenting).

A political party is a collection of individuals who share the same political views. They form national parties to maximize their chances of winning power in general elections.

exam watch

This is an important topic and could be part of any section on the exam paper.

A voluntary organization is a group of people who work voluntarily (without being paid) to raise money to improve conditions or support others. Many voluntary organizations are charities.

A pressure group is a collection of people who aim to influence or change government policy.

A focus group is a collection of people who join together because of a common focus. The focus is usually a local issue.

A trade union is a special type of pressure group which represents the interests of workers in a particular trade or occupation.

A lobbyist is a professional person who is employed to try to influence or change government decisions.

Political parties

The main political parties in Britain are the Conservative Party, the Labour Party and the Liberal Democrats. In Scotland there is the Scottish Nationalist Party, in Wales the Welsh National Party is Plaid Cymru, and in Northern Ireland there are a number of political parties split into three distinct camps – the Unionist parties, the Social Democratic Labour Party and Sinn Fein. Smaller parties include the Green Party, the National Front, the Socialist Party and the UK Independence Party.

All political parties form their own policies and present them to the electorate in a manifesto for a general election, they hope that they will gain power to govern the country and promote changes in society.

Voluntary organizations

Many voluntary organizations are charities, while they may have paid administrative officers the work of raising money is done locally and nationally by volunteers. These organizations work in many areas to:

- raise awareness of conditions in which some people live
- raise money to make situations better
- create activities and opportunities for local people
- create opportunities for young people
- support people in the community.

Pressure groups

Pressure groups usually focus on one area of government policy and this often has an impact locally as well as nationally. They have clear aims which are clearly explained to the public, and they organize campaigns and raise funds to support their cause. Pressure groups seek to influence events and decision making in their sphere of interest in such areas as the environment, human rights, the countryside, education, employment law, discrimination, health and disability rights. Some pressure groups work to promote issues on an international scale and relate to national and European government.

Hints and tips

Make sure you know the main political parties and the names of their leaders, and who is in power locally and nationally.

look back

For more information see pages 52–3 in the textbook.

Hints and tips

You need to know some national and local examples of **voluntary organizations** and some important **pressure groups**, such as Greenpeace and Amnesty International and know a little about what they do. You may have done a case study on one of them.

Focus groups

These are usually local groups of people who join together to concentrate on one community issue such as a school closure. They may take advice from national bodies and when the issue is resolved the group is disbanded.

Trade unions

These represent the interests of workers who are connected through a particular job or trade. Membership of a union does not depend on age, race, gender, religious belief or social status. Trade unions hold regular local meetings with employers and promote such things as health and safety issues, pay and conditions of service and development. Unions also offer legal help and advice to members. As a group the trade unions have one power that no other pressure group has, which is to go on strike or to work to rule.

look back

For more information see pages 55 and 57 of the textbook.

Protests

Peaceful protests have a long history in Britain. They usually take the form of rallies or marches with banners and placards held in major cities, especially London. Sometimes people protest about the same thing and marches are planned for the same day in many towns and cities. The most recent protest like this was about the war with Iraq. This happened on an international scale and was not only a national issue in Britain. This is a case of international co-operation between people not governments.

Another way of protesting peacefully or making the voices of many people heard is to gather a petition and deliver it to the government. Major protests raise the awareness of the general public about the issues involved. Governments usually take the views of peaceful protesters into account when formulating parliamentary debates and reviewing policy.

Pressure groups must choose the technique they are going to use to try to influence public opinion and government action. Sometimes public opinion surveys are specially commissioned to find out the strength of feeling on an issue; or adverts may be placed in the media; or a specific issue will be promoted on a particular day with a lot of publicity; for example, National No-Smoking Day is one Wednesday in March. Whatever method is chosen, care must be taken to keep the protest peaceful and prevent violent protest.

Hints and tips

Make sure you can explain the term **trade union** and can name at least one example.

Action Point (A)

Find out about another recent peaceful protest: what it was about, when it occurred, where and what was the outcome.

Try these short questions

Questions like the ones below will appear in Section A of the exam paper. They require short, factual answers and are worth two marks for each question. Answers to these questions can be found on page 86.

1 List two services local councils are responsible for.
2 How do local councils receive funding? Name two ways.
3 Which voting system is used to elect members to the Welsh Assembly?
4 What was the Jenkins Commission?
5 Name four political parties.
6 What is a pressure group?
7 What does 'CBI' stand for?
8 Name two voluntary organizations.
9 Name two pressure groups.
10 Identify two recent peaceful protests.

Action Point

Test yourself by answering the questions and then looking up the answers. Be honest with yourself – find out what you know and what you still need to learn!

Checklist for revision

	Know and understand	Need more revision	Do not know
Factors affecting community life – ethnic identity, religion, culture	☐	☐	☐
Local government systems	☐	☐	☐
Financing local services	☐	☐	☐
Devolution and regional government	☐	☐	☐
Voting systems	☐	☐	☐
Individuals and change – political parties, voluntary organizations, pressure groups etc.	☐	☐	☐
Protests	☐	☐	☐

exam watch

How many did you get right? Find the right answers to any questions you had wrong or did not fully understand and learn them. Some people find working with a friend and discussing the questions helpful!

National and European citizenship

4 National and European government

What you need to know

- What systems of government operate in the world
- How the democratic system in the UK works
- How national government works
- What the European Union (EU) is about
- What the institutions of the EU are
- The rules of and your part in the democratic process
- How national government manages the economy
- What being part of the EU means to you

Systems of government

Different systems of **government** are in operation across the world.

Republics are led by governments and have no monarch.

One-party states have only one **political party**.

Constitutional monarchies are governed by a group of people elected from a range of political parties and have a monarch as a head of state.

Absolute monarchies are countries ruled by a king or queen who comes from the country's royal family.

Dictatorships are ruled by one person who has authority in all matters.

Key ideas

The UK is a constitutional monarchy. The Queen is the head of state but the power of government is invested in parliament. The UK is a democracy.

The democratic system in the UK

Democracy in the UK has been built over many years. Through its democratic tradition, the UK government hopes to promote participation in the country's decision-making processes.

To be part of the electoral process, that is, to vote in an election, a person must be eighteen years of age and their name must be on the Register of Electors, which is made up by the local council every year.

When an election is called, candidates, who mainly represent various political parties and their views, start their election campaign. Each candidate must be supported by people whose name is on the Register of

Electors. Candidates produce election literature and meet people to ask them to vote for them. Voting takes place at a specified time at a polling station or by postal ballot. Voting is secret.

People elected to serve as local councillors will vote on issues based at a local level: for example, the council tax, housing issues, local environmental issues including **Agenda 21**. Each person is elected for a period of four years. They represent the people in a ward of the council.

People elected as MPs serve for a period of up to five years. They are elected to represent the people in their constituency. They will vote on issues relating to national issues, including:

- taxes
- health
- law and order
- international affairs
- education
- defence
- home affairs
- aid.

How national government works

The government of the UK is undertaken by parliament. Parliament is arranged into two chambers:

- the House of Commons (the lower chamber). The House of Commons makes the laws by which the country is governed and managed
- the House of Lords (the upper chamber) has existed as part of the government since the 1300s.

  The House of Lords:
  - debates issues of national importance that have not been debated in the House of Commons
  - considers bills that have been passed through the reading stages of the House of Commons
  - proposes amendments to bills where appropriate
  - is the final court of appeal in the British judicial system.

Issues of national interest are debated in parliament. At the end of each debate there is a vote to decide who is for the motion (the ayes) and who is against the motion (the nos). At the end of the vote the Speaker will announce the result.

Some work in parliament is done by committees. Select committees meet regularly to deal with routine issues. Standing committees meet for a limited time and deal with specific issues. Some work is done by the Cabinet – a group of senior ministers who meet to decide the government's policy on issues and events. It decides how issues will be dealt with and who will speak for the government on important events.

Key ideas

Laws made by parliament become the law of the land.

Action Point Ⓐ

Name five political parties. Write a list of three polices that each one believes in. For example, the Labour Party believes in: 1) investment in education; 2) reducing hospital waiting lists and patient choice and 3) joining the single currency when it is right for the UK.

Action Point Ⓐ

Name four members of the cabinet and their position. For example, Tony Blair, the Prime Minister.

The European Union

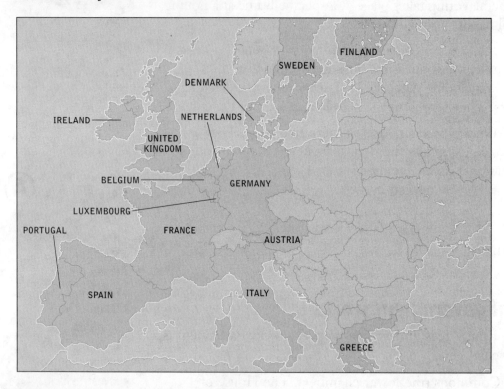

The fifteen member
states of the
European Union

The **European Union (EU)** is made up of fifteen countries known as
member states. To be a member of the EU, countries must meet set
criteria:

- their system of government must be democratic
- they must respect human rights
- they must operate a market economy which matches the economies of
  existing EU member states
- they must support the aims and objectives of the EU with respect to
  market activities.

The EU was first known as the European Economic Community (EEC).
It was created to form a common market where labour, goods and services
could be freely traded. It had six members when it started in 1957. The
UK joined in 1973.

The EU is led by the European Council. The European Council is a
summit meeting usually held twice a year. The summit meeting is where
the heads of government of each member state meet.

The institutions of the EU

The five institutions of the EU are:

- The Council of Ministers
- The European Commission

- The European Parliament
- The European Court of Justice
- The European Court of Auditors.

The Council of Ministers is the main decision-making body of the EU. It is made up of one representative from each member state. The UK is represented by the Foreign Secretary. Decisions are made by a straight majority vote.

The European Commission is based in Brussels. Its main functions are to propose policies and draft laws, ensure that member states uphold EU treaties and implement EU policies, and manage the EU's administration. The EU has 20 commissioners. Each country appoints one commissioner. Italy, France, Spain, Germany and the UK have two commissioners. Commissioners are expected to act independently of their national government.

The European Parliament meets in Strasbourg and Brussels. Representatives are elected to serve for a maximum of five years and are called Members of the European Parliament (MEPs). There are 626 MEPs. Since 1999, MEPs have been elected using proportional representation. A European constituency is larger than a national government constituency. The main function of the European parliament is to debate issues and proposals raised by the European Commission. It is funded by contributions from member states.

The European Court of Justice is located in Luxembourg. The court has 15 judges, one from each member country. The court sits to consider disputes about EU laws. The European court has the power to rule against a decision of a national government.

The European Court of Auditors is the institution which monitors the financial management of the EU. It makes sure that EU finance is being used for the purposes for which it was raised. This court is made up of fifteen members, one from each member country.

Taking part in the democratic process

Elections

One of the most important rights given to someone living in a democracy is the right to be part of a democratic process – in short, to vote on who will govern you. With this right comes responsibility. In the UK the responsibility of voting in elections is optional. There is no penalty if you do not vote. In some countries, like Australia, you are fined if you fail to vote in an election. The number of people voting in local and national elections in the UK has dropped to low levels. There has been much debate about the reasons for this decline and some areas have introduced postal voting as a means of increasing the number of people who vote.

Action Point

Name as many of the EU member states as you can. Then, use the map on page 24 to help you with the ones you have forgotten.

Everyone in the year in that they become eighteen is invited to add their name to the Register of Electors. This register tells the returning officer (the person in charge of the conduct of elections) who is eligible to vote in an election. Members of the House of Lords and convicted prisoners are not allowed to vote. When an election is called a date is set for polling to take place.

The polling station is supervised by polling clerks who make sure that the ballot is held in secret and that each person receives a stamped ballot paper on which they mark a cross against the name of their chosen candidate.

To be a candidate in an election, you must be a British citizen and 21 years of age or over. People who cannot stand as candidates for election include:

- some members of the Roman Catholic and Anglican clergy
- members of the House of Lords
- civil servants
- judges
- members of the armed services
- the police.

A candidate must be supported by ten registered voters who live in the constituency. Each candidate pays a deposit of £500 to the returning officer which is lost if they do not secure 5 per cent of the votes cast in their election. The returning officer publishes the list of candidates and issues the date of polling.

People who cannot vote in person can apply for a postal vote or a proxy vote. If you have a proxy vote, someone will go to the polling station and vote on your behalf. If you vote by post, you will fill in a form and send it to the returning officer. Postal votes are opened in front of the candidates when the votes for the election are counted.

Referenda

If there is an issue of national importance that will affect people's lives, some countries hold a referendum to find out what people think. Switzerland is one country that uses referenda regularly to find out the opinion of its citizens. Britain held a referendum in 1975 to decide whether or not the country should continue as a member of the Common Market (EEC). People who support referenda say that the system allows people to make decisions about important issues. People who oppose referenda say that they are expensive to set up, that as few people vote the results would be unsatisfactory and that we should let our elected representatives get on with the job for which they are elected.

Using the Internet

Some people think that consultation with the public could be done on the Internet. They think that this would make consultation quick and efficient. Opponents say that it discriminates against those with no Internet facilities.

did you know?

Men have voted since 1884. Women have had the same rights since 1928.

Key ideas

In a democracy, the government involves people by giving them information so they can make appropriate and informed decisions. A healthy democracy involves people in debate and discussion and, where possible, decision-making. To involve all people in the election process, political parties use a range of strategies to advise and inform the electorate; for example, to encourage young people to vote they have enlisted personalities and pop stars to speak on their behalf.

Local council consultations

Local councils consult residents and local people about important issues like school closure and new housing. They consult through meetings and ask for public comment in documents. Some councils keep local people informed about their council through news magazines.

How national government manages the economy

We have already learned that one of the main functions of the government is to raise finance to pay for public spending. The government spends on health, education, defence, police, prisons and many other services. There are fifteen main government departments which rely on public funds to function. Money is raised through a system of taxation.

Direct taxation is the tax paid from the income people earn.

Indirect taxation is the tax raised from taxes like Value Added Tax (VAT). This tax does not depend on what people earn, but is a fixed-rate tax charged on goods and services.

Proportional Tax stays at the same percentage regardless of the money earned. National Insurance Contributions are a type of proportional tax.

look back
Full details of government spending can be found in the textbook in Figure 4.4, page 73.

The budget

Every year the government makes an economic statement about financial matters. This is known as the **budget**. The budget statement, made by the Chancellor of the Exchequer, outlines the spending targets the government has set out for the next year. It will cover items like allowances for children, tax allowances, pension increases, unemployment benefits, etc. Balancing the books, keeping people healthy, happy and safe while caring for the sick, the elderly and the disabled are some of the issues facing the government.

Action Point (A)
Find out the names of the Chancellor of the Exchequer and the Shadow Chancellor of the Exchequer.

Inflation

One way of checking that the government has met its own spending forecasts and targets is checking the level of inflation. The government sets targets for inflation and it must keep inflation under control. If the level of inflation is high, then prices go up and goods become too expensive for ordinary people. If inflation falls too low, then the economy might slow down and a depression may follow. This could lead to job losses and less money to spend. It is important that the government gets these spending targets right.

look back
The stages a bill goes through to become an act are on page 87 of the textbook

Controlling government spending

The House of Commons has a duty to make sure that the government does not raise money through taxation without good cause. The budget proposals are presented to parliament as a Finance Bill. The bill passes through the same stages as any bill. Making a Finance Bill and Act takes about four months. This gives parliament plenty of time to discuss the proposals. Once the act has come into force, the Public Accounts Committee checks that each department has spent the money on the programmes for which it was raised.

Becoming a European citizen

One of the areas where there is some disagreement in the EU is membership of the single currency. In July 2002, the euro became the sole unit of currency in thirteen member states of the EU. Although all EU countries qualify for membership of the single currency, Britain and Denmark chose not to join. Even though Britain is not a member of the single currency, the euro is accepted in shops throughout the UK. People who are for the single currency point out that the euro would give greater stability to industry if there were no costs attached to the exchange rate. Opponents say that Britain would lose control of its own finances if decisions were made centrally in Europe.

The EU budget is set by the European Parliament and the Council of Ministers. Some countries, for example, Greece, Portugal and Ireland, receive more from the EU than they contribute. The UK and Germany are two of the countries that put more money in than they get out. Each member state gives some of its country's revenue to the EU. The EU then sets targets for spending and allocates the finance to meet these targets. In 1993 the UK gave 0.9 per cent of its Gross National Product (GNP) to the EU.

The EU affects the average citizen in many ways. Its commissioners are preparing reports for consultation and discussion on a wide range of issues which influence the lives of all EU citizens. These include:

- The EU Commission on Human Rights upholds the rights of individuals and groups. The rights are laid down in the **European Convention on Human Rights**. The commission is made up of judges who hear issues raised by any individual or group who feel that their human rights have been neglected or violated.
- As an EU citizen, it is easier to travel, work and study in Europe.
- The EU has a set of rules that apply to consumer goods.
- The EU has standards for food labelling.
- There are safety regulations attached to toys and electrical goods.
- The EU funds projects in poorer regions to develop regional economies.
- The EU has a range of development projects to improve the environment; for example, reducing air pollution, basic water and bathing standards, noise emissions in the community and workplace.

Action Point Ⓐ

Name five of the government departments that the Public Accounts Committee monitors.

Action Point Ⓐ

Write a definition of GNP.

Try these short questions

Questions like the ones below will appear in Section A of the exam paper. They require short, factual answers and are worth two marks for each question. Answers to these questions can be found on page 86.

1 Name three systems of government.
2 How often is the Register of Electors compiled?
3 Name the two Houses of the British Parliament.
4 What is the Cabinet?
5 What does 'EU' stand for?
6 How old do you have to be to stand for election as an MP in Britain?
7 Name two types of taxation.
8 Which committee checks government spending?
9 Name two institutions of the EU.
10 What is a proxy vote?

Action Point **A**

Test yourself by answering the questions and then looking up the answers. Be honest with yourself – find out what you know and what you still need to learn!

Checklist for revision

	Know and understand	Need more revision	Do not know
I know what systems of government operate in the world	☐	☐	☐
I know how the democratic system in the UK works	☐	☐	☐
I know how national government works	☐	☐	☐
I know what the EU is about	☐	☐	☐
I know what the institutions of the EU are	☐	☐	☐
I know the rules of and my part in the democratic process	☐	☐	☐
I know how national government manages the economy	☐	☐	☐
I know what being part of the EU means to me	☐	☐	☐

exam watch

How many did you get right? Some people find making revision FLASH cards helpful.

5 Criminal and civil law

What you need to know

- How the law affects you
- How the law affects consumers
- What work young people are allowed to do
- How the law deals with discrimination
- What crime is and how we guard against it
- What the police are allowed to do
- How a law is made
- European laws
- What civil and criminal law are
- How different courts work
- What happens at the European Court
- Who works in the legal system

How the law affects you

The law restricts what you can do until you are an adult, when it expects you to accept full responsibility for your own actions. The figure on page 31 shows what you can do at certain ages.

Laws affect every aspect of our lives. They:
- protect lives and property.
- set standards of acceptable behaviour.
- set standards for food, water, air and hygiene.
- lay down the punishment for breaking society's rules.

Society has its laws set by parliament, but each organization has a set of rules or code of conduct for its members.

Parents' duties

While there are laws governing how society expects children to be treated, many of the rules governing how your parents treat you are parental responsibilities rather than laws. They tell parents what expectations society has for the care of children. Until you are an adult, your parents are expected to look after you. They should:

Action Point Ⓐ

Look at the figure on page 31 carefully. Do you think that the law has these ages correct? What would you change, if any, and why?

- make sure that you are properly fed and clothed
- take you for medical treatment if you are ill
- make sure that you receive a proper education
- discipline you and decide how to punish you.

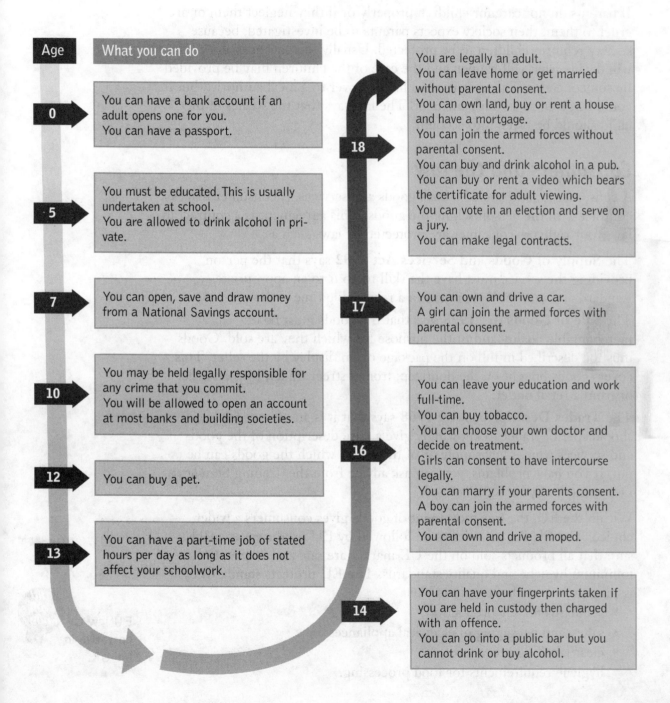

Age	What you can do
0	You can have a bank account if an adult opens one for you. You can have a passport.
5	You must be educated. This is usually undertaken at school. You are allowed to drink alcohol in private.
7	You can open, save and draw money from a National Savings account.
10	You may be held legally responsible for any crime that you commit. You will be allowed to open an account at most banks and building societies.
12	You can buy a pet.
13	You can have a part-time job of stated hours per day as long as it does not affect your schoolwork.
14	You can have your fingerprints taken if you are held in custody then charged with an offence. You can go into a public bar but you cannot drink or buy alcohol.
16	You can leave your education and work full-time. You can buy tobacco. You can choose your own doctor and decide on treatment. Girls can consent to have intercourse legally. You can marry if your parents consent. A boy can join the armed forces with parental consent. You can own and drive a moped.
17	You can own and drive a car. A girl can join the armed forces with parental consent.
18	You are legally an adult. You can leave home or get married without parental consent. You can own land, buy or rent a house and have a mortgage. You can join the armed forces without parental consent. You can buy and drink alcohol in a pub. You can buy or rent a video which bears the certificate for adult viewing. You can vote in an election and serve on a jury. You can make legal contracts.

What the law allows you to do, from 0–18

Parents also have rights. They have the right to:

- determine which medical treatment you will receive
- decide how you will be educated and which school, if any, you will attend
- decide which religion you will follow until you are old enough to decide for yourself.

If parents do not care for children properly or if they neglect them or are cruel to them, then society expects parents to be investigated, because society requires children to be protected. Usually this means that a court will decide what will happen and the care of the children may be provided by someone else. This care is often handed over to a local authority, but it could be given to a family member. The law says that the wishes of the child should be taken into account.

Consumers and the law

A consumer is someone who buys goods and services. A consumer makes a contract with the person selling the goods. This agreement is a contract in law. Your rights as consumer are protected by laws such as:

The **Supply of Goods and Services Act 1982** says that the person providing the service must have the skill to do it to an appropriate standard and must provide it within a reasonable time-scale.

The **Sale of Goods Act 1978** says that the goods must be of merchantable quality and fit the purpose for which they are sold. Goods must be described in full on the package or on display by the seller. This covers goods bought on the doorstep, from a street trader, by mail order or from a retail outlet.

The **Trades Descriptions Act 1968** says that it is an offence for a shopkeeper or trader to knowingly give a false description of the goods and services which they supply or of the use to which the goods can be put. If you have problems, you can ask advice from the Trading Standards Department of your local council.

Within the EU, the free movement of goods gives consumers a wider choice. The EU has set rules to be followed by EU producers to make sure that all products sold on the UK market are safe and respect the minimum hygiene and quality standards. The EU protects standards by issuing directives about matters like:

- standards for toy production
- safety and packaging of electrical appliances
- clear labelling procedures
- hygiene requirements for food processing.

EU law is operative in the UK.

Young people and employment

> The law determines what a young person can do and how long they can work at different ages. In all cases, any employment undertaken must not interfere with schoolwork, so a young person should ask permission of their school before undertaking employment. The rules governing working hours will be available from a local careers office.

Until a person is thirteen, they can only be employed by a special licence in the entertainment industry or do jobs at home for their parents including agricultural work. Young people may work full time from the age of sixteen.

The law and discrimination

Everyone has equal rights under the law. So the law protects people from discrimination on the grounds of race, sex or disability.

Direct discrimination means that a person has been treated less favourably than their direct counterpart.

Indirect discrimination occurs when the conditions required for a job cannot be applied equally to all potential applicants.

look back
For further details see pages 83–4 in the textbook.

UK law is clear about types of discrimination and there are acts to protect people:

- The **Race Relations Act 1976** came into being to prevent racial discrimination. It is illegal to discriminate on the grounds of colour or ethnic origin in matters relating to employment, education, housing and the provision of goods and services.
- The **Sex Discrimination Acts 1975 and 1986** make it unlawful to treat anyone on the grounds of their sex less favourably than a person of the opposite sex. This can relate to hours worked, quality of jobs given and payment made.
- The **Disability Discrimination Act 1995** makes it illegal to discriminate against someone with a disability in matters relating to employment, education, training, housing, public services and transport.

The EU produced the **Social Charter** to improve the living and working conditions of EU workers. This charter states the fundamental rights of workers. It includes:

- employment rights for temporary and part-time workers including rest periods and holiday pay
- equal pay for equal work
- improved professional integration for disabled people
- health and safety protection.

What is crime?

If something is unlawful or illegal, then it is an offence against the law of the land. This means that it is a **crime**. There are two main types of crime: crime which involves people and crime which involves property. Crimes against people include assault, rape and murder. Crimes against property include arson and vandalism. The reasons why people commit crimes are complex. The number of crimes being committed is increasing. There are many reasons for this. They include:

- the growth of materialism
- the breakdown in family life
- the loss of the extended family system
- unemployment
- drinking and drug-taking
- activities on film and television.

The role of the police

The police force is the public's defence against crime and the criminal. The police force's main duties are to:

- prevent and detect crime
- protect life and property
- maintain public order.

The duties and powers of the police force are set out in the **Police and Criminal Evidence Act 1984**. This act also makes sure that the police operate within the law. Police officers will be disciplined if they:

- neglect their duty
- make a false accusation
- misuse their authority
- are abusive to a member of the public
- display racial discrimination.

If you wish to complain about any aspect of police operation or conduct, you can get information from the Police Complaints Authority.

The police need the public to help them by reporting crimes and acting as witnesses. If the police stop and search you, then you are suspected of carrying stolen goods, drugs, weapons or tools for burglary. Anyone who is stopped and searched should know what the police expect to find. From time to time people are asked to help the police with their enquiries. Helping the police does not always mean that the person being questioned is accused of the offence.

However, if you are arrested and charged with an offence, you may be:

- **reprimanded or given a caution**. Only people who admit that they have broken the law can be reprimanded or cautioned.
- **prosecuted.** Your case will be referred to a court for consideration.

If you are found guilty of a crime, your details will be stored on the Police National Computer and you will have a criminal record.

Law-making in action

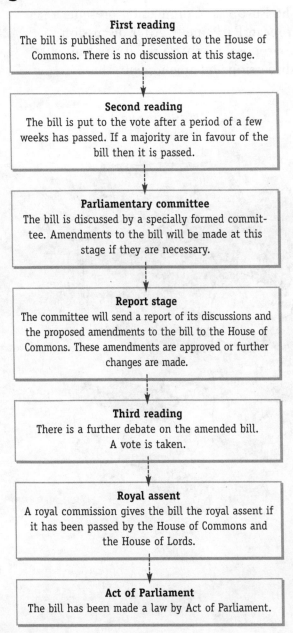

First reading
The bill is published and presented to the House of Commons. There is no discussion at this stage.

Second reading
The bill is put to the vote after a period of a few weeks has passed. If a majority are in favour of the bill then it is passed.

Parliamentary committee
The bill is discussed by a specially formed committee. Amendments to the bill will be made at this stage if they are necessary.

Report stage
The committee will send a report of its discussions and the proposed amendments to the bill to the House of Commons. These amendments are approved or further changes are made.

Third reading
There is a further debate on the amended bill. A vote is taken.

Royal assent
A royal commission gives the bill the royal assent if it has been passed by the House of Commons and the House of Lords.

Act of Parliament
The bill has been made a law by Act of Parliament.

How laws are made

The laws in Britain have been made over many years in a variety of ways.

Statutes are the laws that have been made by parliament.

Common law includes laws that have been passed down through the ages.

By-laws have been made by local councils and public agencies to deal with local issues such as litter and dog fouling.

Case law is where a judge will make a decision about any issues presented to court after previous, similar cases have been explored.

European laws

Laws are also made in the EU. The European Commission presents a proposal for discussion in the European Parliament. After discussion, amendment and redrafting, a firm proposal is sent to the European Council for consideration. After discussion and amendment, the European Council members will seek the advice of their national governments. When agreement is reached, the proposal is returned to the European Parliament. If the European Parliament approves the proposal, the European Council adopts it as European law. European laws are binding on all member countries and are known as EU regulations. An EU directive instructs member states to introduce a new law within a set time limit.

Criminal and civil law

In Britain there are two types of law. **Civil law** relates to a person's private rights; for example, boundary disputes and marital breakdown. **Criminal law** relates to crimes which are against the law of the land. Criminal law is enforced by the police and Crown Prosecution Service. Each set of laws is heard in its own court system. Each type of court has its own procedure and practice.

How different courts work

Civil law

Because civil law relates to disputes concerning contracts or agreements with another person over a private matter, the matter is often dealt with by the court without the people being present. Civil cases are referred to county courts for consideration. In these cases, one person (the plaintiff) takes action against another person (the defendant). The plaintiff is said to be suing the defendant. The court will consider the case and make a judgement of 'liable' or 'not liable'. If the defendant is liable, then they are likely to have to pay damages (compensation) to the plaintiff. In a county court the judge decides on the outcome. If the case deals with a lot of money, a complex financial issue or a contested custody case, then the issue will be referred to the relevant branch of the High Court.

For more details see page 90 of the textbook.

Criminal law

Criminal law relates to matters such as theft, assault, drug offences, violence and murder. Because these offences are against the law, offenders are prosecuted by the Crown Prosecution Service (CPS). The CPS aims to protect individuals and society against crime. The majority of criminal cases are heard in magistrates' courts. Magistrates sit in a panel of three people. They are given advice by the clerk to the court. Magistrates have a list of sentences set for different types of offence. Some cases heard in the magistrates' court will be referred to a crown court for trial, judgement and sentence.

The maximum sentence in a magistrates' court is a £5000 fine or six months in prison.

When a criminal case is held at a crown court, it is heard by a judge and jury. The jury has twelve members. Usually the defendant has pleaded 'not guilty'. During the trial, the prosecution puts its case, presents evidence and, where appropriate, calls witnesses. This process is repeated by the defence. The judge will then sum up the case and the jury will retire to consider the case. The jury returns to court and the verdict is announced by the foreman of the jury. If the accused is found guilty, the judge will pronounce the sentence. If the accused is found not guilty, the judge will discharge the case.

There are special courts to deal with children aged 10–18. These are called youth courts. Members of the public are not allowed into youth court and the defendant cannot be named in any press coverage. Parents must accompany children up to the age of 16. Cases at youth courts are heard by specially trained magistrates.

What happens at the European Court

The European Court of Justice was set up in 1952 and enlarged in 1989. Its job is to ensure that EU law is correctly observed. This court rules on the laws of the EU and interprets it for member countries. The Court of Justice takes action where countries fail to act on European rulings or fail to fulfil treaty obligations.

People in the legal system

Many people work in the legal system in Britain. Here are details of some of them.

Magistrates are ordinary citizens who are appointed to sit in judgement. They are known as Justices of the Peace (JPs). They work part time and are unpaid. Magistrates receive training to undertake their role.

Judges are highly qualified barristers or solicitors who are nominated or appointed by the Lord Chancellor. They hold full-time appointments and are paid for their work.

Barristers are specialists in advocacy and the law. They present a client's case to a court or tribunal. They ask questions in court.

Solicitors work in private practice, for local authorities, large organizations, industry and commerce. They give legal advice relating to a wide area of law from matrimonial issues to land searches, and represent clients in court.

A **Clerk to the Court** is a full-time, paid officer of the court who gives advice to magistrates on points of law.

Ushers are paid officers of the court who organize the smooth running of the court. They arrange for witnesses to be called at the correct time.

A **Jury** is selected randomly from the current electoral register. To be on a jury, you must be over 18 and under 70.

Try these short questions

Questions like the ones below will appear in Section A of the exam paper. They require short, factual answers and are worth two marks for each question. Answers to these questions can be found on page 87.

1 Name two things your parents have the right to choose for you.
2 What is a consumer?
3 Name one act affecting consumers, and say when it was passed.
4 Name the department of the local council that deals with consumer affairs.
5 List two types of crime against people.
6 Who would you complain to about the police?
7 Name two types of law.
8 What type of law is dealt with in a) crown court, b) county court?
9 In court, who helps magistrates with points of law?
10 How many people make up a jury?

Action Point Ⓐ

Test yourself by answering the questions and then looking up the answers. Be honest with yourself – find out what you know and what you still need to learn!

Checklist for revision

	Know and understand	Need more revision	Do not know
I know how the law affects me	☐	☐	☐
I know how the law affects consumers	☐	☐	☐
I know what work young people are allowed to do	☐	☐	☐
I know how the law deals with discrimination	☐	☐	☐
I know what crime is and how we guard against it	☐	☐	☐
I know what the police are allowed to do	☐	☐	☐
I know how a law is made	☐	☐	☐
I know what civil and criminal law are	☐	☐	☐
I know about European laws	☐	☐	☐
I know how different courts work	☐	☐	☐
I know who works in the legal system	☐	☐	☐
I know what happens at the European Court	☐	☐	☐

exam watch

How many did you get right? Some people find it helps to turn the revision into a *quiz game*. Try this with a few revision mates!

6 The media

What you need to know

- How much the media influences our lives
- How the media is organized
- How the media is monitored
- The influence of television
- The influence of new technology
- How advertising affects our lives

How much does the media influence our lives?

The **media**, sometimes called the mass media, is the means by which you can communicate with a large number of people at the same time. Television, magazines, newspapers, radio, books, video, advertisements, film and the Internet are parts of the mass media. We are exposed to the media in one form or another from a very early age. The media influences our thoughts, our attitudes, our actions and, in some cases, our behaviour.

Article 19 of the United Nations Universal Declaration of Human Rights gives everyone the freedom to hold their own opinions and to express them (**freedom of speech**). Freedom of the press allows news agencies to publish stories and information as long as these stories are legal. In some countries the state controls the content in newspapers and magazines. Where the news sources are controlled by the state, the content is often censored. This means that the paper can only print what the state wants people to read. Sometimes information is circulated which is designed to influence people. This is known as propaganda. Propaganda can be spread using different media. The Nazi party used film and radio very successfully to spread its message.

Sometimes the government or a large organization wants to control the public response to an issue by presenting the information in a certain way. To do this the information is 'moved around' to highlight one section and minimize another. This movement is giving the information a spin. People who are employed to undertake this job are called spin doctors. Spin doctors use a range of techniques to control the amount of information handed to the press at any time.

Action Point

Name two countries where the state controls the newspapers.

How the media is organized

The UK has a wide range of national, regional and local newspapers. New technology means that stories and pictures can be changed quickly as events happen. Newspapers know that they can appeal to different audiences so they choose their headlines, photographs and language carefully. The tabloids (the *Mirror*, the *Sun*) are sometimes called the popular press. The broadsheet newspapers (*The Guardian*, *The Times*) are sometimes called the quality press. Newspapers, like magazines and television companies, are owned by large companies. Sometimes individual people own media companies. We call these people media barons. Rupert Murdoch is a media baron. He is the head of News International, which owns Sky television, the *Sun*, *The Times* and other companies.

Some people are concerned that a small number of people are controlling the news services and that the news is not fully representative of the world, particularly the developing countries. They often feel that the media is very influential in moulding public opinion and the media is not free from bias.

How the media is monitored

The media in the UK is monitored by two bodies. Their role is to control the standards of reporting information to the public. These bodies monitor television, advertising and press coverage of events. The Radio Authority monitors coverage on the radio.

The Press Complaints Commission (PCC) monitors publications. There is a code of practice which newspapers and magazines must follow when publishing. The code covers many issues. These say that:

Action Point Ⓐ

Make a list of three tabloid and three broadsheet newspapers.

look back

For more information on the PCC and the influence of the media look at pages 99–100 in the textbook

VOICE OF THE Mirror

Don't play Saddam's mad game

From the *Daily Mirror*, 13 March 2002

BLOODY DANGEROUS

By JAMES HARDY — EU's fear on Iraq attack

From the *Daily Mirror*, 16 March 2002

Blair woos summit amid fears of split

Ian Black in Barcelona

From *The Guardian*, 16 March 2002

Newspaper headlines of the same story

- all printed material must be accurate
- individuals and organizations must have the right to reply
- individuals should have their private life, home, health and correspondence respected
- journalists and photographers must not intimidate individuals
- children must be protected and should not have their education disturbed.

The PCC considers all complaints where individuals and organizations argue that the code of practice was not upheld. Complaints relating to television are considered by the Independent Television Authority (ITA).

The influence of television

Perhaps the greatest influence on people's lives is made by television. The average Briton watches television for three hours every day. People say that television:

- defines what we should think, what we should buy, what success is, what makes us happy, how we should behave
- can distort our view of reality
- concentrates on values based on wealth, power, physical beauty and strength and has reduced children's ability to create imaginative games.

As a strong and powerful tool in society, television must reinforce the best ideals and values.

did you know?

That terrestrial news channels in the UK must be politically neutral.

The influence of new technology

Another powerful tool is the Internet. The Internet along with other digital electronic technologies, such as interactive television and CD ROM, are known as the new media or new technologies. The ease and speed of access of information on the Internet causes concern because there is no control over the transmission of sensitive material, including security details and pornographic material. Also there is no control over the transmission of false or libellous information. As a result, individual's rights may be violated. New technology allows the immediate transfer of photographs and information from across the globe. New video telephone connections allow us to see and hear news correspondents deliver information as they receive it. This immediacy makes it even more important that facts are transmitted correctly because this reality television can be emotive and hugely influential in formulating opinion.

Action Point (A)

Make a list of five things that cannot be controlled on the Internet.

How are we influenced by advertising?

Advertising is everywhere. We can hear it on the radio and see it on the television, at the cinema, on billboards and in the newspapers and magazines. Manufacturers spend large amounts of money advertising their goods. Independent radio and television companies fund their programmes with the money from advertising and sponsorship.

Action Point (A)

Name three celebrities who advertise products and name the product they advertise.

Some people think that advertisements are a waste of money because they don't influence people, whereas other people think that advertising makes people buy things that they don't want or need. There is a belief that adverts exaggerate the quality or range of the products by using humour or celebrities to encourage people to buy. Many adverts are targeted at young people to encourage them to buy designer and high-priced goods. These adverts create a specific lifestyle that young people subscribe to and so feel obliged to buy the goods.

Television advertising is regulated by the Independent Television Commission and radio advertising is controlled by the Radio Authority. Advertisements should be honest, decent and truthful. They should not discriminate. For children, advertisements should not include material which 'might result in harm to them either physically, mentally or morally'. The advertising code sets out the rules for advertising on radio and television.

look back
There are fuller details on page 101 of the text book.

Try these short questions

Questions like the ones below will appear in Section A of the exam paper. They require short, factual answers and are worth two marks for each question. Answers to these questions can be found on page 87.

1 What is a spin doctor?
2 Name two tabloid newspapers.
3 Which body monitors what is printed in the press?
4 Name two broadsheet newspapers.
5 What is a media baron?
6 What does the Independent Television Commission do?
7 Name two qualities a television advert should comply with?
8 What is meant by propaganda?

Action Point (A)

Test yourself by answering the questions and then looking up the answers. Be honest with yourself – find out what you know and what you still need to learn!

Checklist for revision

	Know and understand	Need more revision	Do not know
I know how much the media influences our lives	☐	☐	☐
I know how the media is organized	☐	☐	☐
I know how the media is monitored	☐	☐	☐
I know how advertising affects our lives	☐	☐	☐
I know how television influences us	☐	☐	☐
I know how new technology influences us	☐	☐	☐

exam watch

How many did you get right? Some people find working with a friend and discussing the questions helpful.

7 International relations

> **What you need to know**
>
> - The UK and its international relations
> - The UK and the Commonwealth
> - What the UN is and what it stands for
> - How the UN is organized
> - The role of the UN in the modern world
> - The UK and NATO
> - The UK, conflict and co-operation

For centuries, the nation state was central to international relations across the world. Each country controlled its own goods and services, so the economy of each country was a distinct entity. As world trade has increased and new technology has made communication easier, countries now share experiences and trade with each other. This has led to the growth of organizations with common aims and hopes.

The UK and international relations

The UK is a member of the **European Union**, the **United Nations**, the **Commonwealth** and **NATO**. Because it is a member of all these organizations, the UK often has to tread a careful diplomatic path so it does not damage relationships with one or other of these organizations. The war in Iraq which started in March 2003 has caused tension for the UK within the UN and the EU.

The UK and the Commonwealth

The Commonwealth was created in 1931 to support free trade between member countries. It consists of 54 sovereign nations and dependencies. Many of the member countries were formerly part of the British Empire. However, Mozambique, which is a member, used to be a Portuguese colony. Canada, Australia, New Zealand and the UK have remained Commonwealth partners since 1931. They have worked together in co-operative ventures since then. The Heads of State from Commonwealth countries meet every two years for a conference (Commonwealth Heads of Government Meeting – CHOGM) and every four years athletes from Commonwealth countries compete in the Commonwealth Games. Britain gives over 50 per cent of its foreign aid to Commonwealth countries.

did you know?

HRH the Queen is head of the Commonwealth.

Action Point (A)

Name ten members of the Commonwealth.

The United Nations

The **United Nations** (UN) aims to promote international peace, security and co-operation. The UK was one of the founder members of the UN. There are 185 countries in the UN. Each member country must contribute a minimum of 0.1 per cent of the UN budget. The budget is paid in US dollars.

How the UN is organized

The UN is governed by the **United Nations Charter**. All member states must sign the Charter, which outlines the aims and objectives of the UN. These include:

- the maintenance of international peace and security
- arms control
- the protection of human rights
- the giving of aid to refugees and famine victims.

There are guidelines, statements and resolutions telling people what procedures and practices should be adopted and acted on.

The **UN Secretariat** is based in New York and is headed by the Secretary-General of the United Nations who is responsible for running the UN.

The **UN General Assembly** meets annually and each of the 185 members of the UN is represented. For a decision to be made, two-thirds of the members must be in favour.

The **UN Security Council** was set up after World War II. The Council has five permanent members and ten temporary members. The five permanent members have the right to veto any resolution placed before the Council. There must be a majority for a resolution to be passed. The UN Security Council deals with:

- threats to international security
- the arms trade
- weapons of mass destruction
- UN peacekeeping forces.

The Security Council suggests what action should be taken when a country fails to comply with a UN resolution.

The role of the UN in the modern world

The United Nations works to improve the living and working conditions of people throughout the world. It has organizations dealing with children, health, trade, aid, food, population, development and finance. It works with member states individually and jointly in a spirit of friendly support, negotiation and co-operation.

did you know?

Zimbabwe (2002), Fiji (2000), Nigeria (1993) South Africa (1961–94) have been suspended from the Commonwealth.

Action Point (A)

Name the Secretary-General of the UN and the five permanent members of the Security Council.

look back

Fuller details can be found on page 111 of the text book.

The UN provides peacekeeping forces at times of conflict or disorder in a country by asking member states to provide defence troops from their armed forces to form a peacekeeping force. The UK has worked as a UN peacekeeper in Bosnia, Sierra Leone and Afghanistan. Being part of a peacekeeping force is not without risk. During a period of five years, 60 British personnel lost their lives undertaking peacekeeping duties.

Another UN organization is the **United Nations Environment Programme (UNEP)**, which was set up to safeguard the global environment for future generations. The programme deals with:

- support for UNEP Agenda 21
- research into global warming and **acid rain**
- the types and number of plants and animal species in different parts of the world and guards them against extinction.

The programme works with non-government organizations (NGOs) such as Greenpeace and Friends of the Earth to implement its programmes.

The **United Nations Commission on Human Rights** is responsible for monitoring the operation of the Universal Declaration of Human Rights. The commission monitors countries for human rights abuses such as torture and discrimination. It reports its findings to the UN General Assembly. The commission works with NGOs such as Amnesty International to improve human rights across the world.

The UK and NATO

The **North Atlantic Treaty Organization (NATO)** was created in 1949 as an alliance of twelve nations committed to each others' defence. The UK was a founder member. By 1999 the total number of countries involved in the alliance was nineteen.

NATO provides:
- defence for any member country against the threat of aggression
- a key role in crisis management and conflict prevention
- a commitment to promoting partnership and co-operation with other countries to increase understanding and respect
- leadership of the multinational force in Kosovo, Bosnia and hopes that its involvement will create a strong, democratic society and a lasting peace.

Action Point
Name five members of NATO.

NATO countries meet regularly to discuss issues of joint interest and concern and to plan future areas of co-operation. The armed forces of the member countries join together to undertake planned military exercises. This builds trust, confidence and understanding to enable military units to work together. This political and military co-operation has allowed NATO to meet its objectives over the last 50 years.

The UK, conflict and co-operation

In recent years, the UK has been involved in several disputes with other countries. Each of these disputes required diplomatic involvement in negotiations with the other countries. Here are two very different examples of British involvement in conflict.

1 In 1982, Britain engaged in military conflict with Argentina because the Argentines invaded the Falkland Islands, a British dependency. The Argentines surrendered after an intense military campaign where men and ships were lost on both sides. The Falkland Islanders wish to remain British so a military presence remains on the islands.

2 In 1713, Gibraltar was given to the British and it has been a military base at the entrance to the Mediterranean for many years. Spain would like to have the sovereignty of Gibraltar handed back to them but the people of Gibraltar wish to remain a part of Britain. Talks have taken place between Spain and Britain but this remains an unresolved issue.

There are many reasons why conflict takes place. Sometimes a small argument can escalate into a major dispute because:

- a clear leader is not evident
- the leadership of the group is challenged
- groups with opposing views refuse to negotiate
- one group refuses to resolve the issue
- the physically stronger group decides to impose its power.

It is difficult to resolve any conflict without compromise and negotiation. Without both parties in an argument agreeing to consider the other's position, there is little chance of a way forward being found.

One dispute that has moved closer to a successful resolution through negotiation, co-operation and compromise is the long running conflict in Northern Ireland. The 1998 Good Friday Agreement was signed by the political parties of Northern Ireland, Eire and the UK. This agreement is a framework for the peaceful settlement of this conflict and was achieved after years of discussion and co-operation.

Try these short questions

Questions like the ones below will appear in Section A of the exam paper. They require short, factual answers and are worth two marks for each question. Answers to these questions can be found on page 87.

1   What does 'NATO' stand for?
2   Name two countries that have been in the Commonwealth since it started.
3   Who is the head of the Commonwealth?
4   Who is the Secretary-General of the United Nations?
5   Where is the headquarters of the UN?
6   How many countries are members of NATO?
7   How often are the Commonwealth Games held?
8   Name two areas of conflict that the UK has been involved in.

Action Point (A)

Test yourself by answering the questions and then looking up the answers. Be honest with yourself – find out what you know and what you still need to learn!

Checklist for revision

	Know and understand	Need more revision	Do not know
I know about the UK and its international relations	☐	☐	☐
I know about the UK and the Commonwealth	☐	☐	☐
I know what the UN is and what it stands for	☐	☐	☐
I know how the UN is organized	☐	☐	☐
I understand the role of the UN in the modern world	☐	☐	☐
I know about the UK and NATO	☐	☐	☐
I know about the UK, conflict and co-operation	☐	☐	☐

exam watch

How many did you get right? Some people find creating revision MIND MAPS helpful.

8 World trade and overseas aid

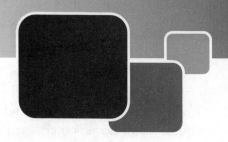

What you need to know

- The basis of global inequality
- What LEDCs and MEDCs are
- What the World Trade Organization is and what it does
- What free trade and fair trade agreements are
- What a multinational company is
- The impact of multinational companies
- What aid is and how it is used
- What sustainable development is
- How Agenda 21 aims to protect for the future

Global inequality

In simple terms, the world is divided into two halves – the wealthy North and the poorer South. Two-thirds of the world's population live in poverty while the remaining third enjoys a large proportion of the world's wealth. This is known as the **development gap**.

More Economically Developed Countries (MEDCs)

The most powerful countries in the world are those that are rich through having a developed economy. Many of these countries are in western Europe. Together with North America, they have shared aspirations and social and political values. These countries have undergone industrial and social change that has led to economic and technological development. They are known as First World countries and have low birth rates, low death rates, low infant mortality rates and high life expectancy. These countries have a strong infrastructure including transport, communications and public health systems. They are known as More Economically Developed Countries (MEDCs).

look back A fuller report on this is on pages 121–3 of the textbook.

Less Economically Developed Countries (LEDCs)

Countries where the infrastructure and industry are not fully developed are known as developing or **Third World** countries. It is usual to find high birth rates and high death rates with higher infant mortality rates and lower life expectancy than in developed countries. The economic gap between Third World and First World countries is increasing. Part of the problem is the considerable debts which the Third World countries have amassed and which they are finding difficult to repay. The countries which require major developments are known as Less Economically Developed Countries (LEDCs).

Future change

Closing the development gap will not be a short-term challenge, nor will it be easy. It will require a change in the way the world is organized and managed. The western nations and multinational companies will need to pay an economic rate for the raw materials and labour provided by developing countries instead of maximizing profits at the expense of weaker nations. Although aid packages and investment programmes have helped developing countries, they can only work in a stable environment and the political tensions in some developing countries have not helped economic and social development.

The World Trade Organization

Trade is the movement of goods and services between different areas or countries. Most countries rely on trade as a major source of income. The import and export of goods between countries is regulated by trade agreements. A UN agency called the **World Trade Organization (WTO)** meets to discuss issues about trade and the operation of trade agreements. Countries or companies that feel they are being unfairly treated can refer issues to the World Trade Organization.

Free trade and fair agreements

Many countries belong to **free trade** associations and other trading groups. The main aim of trading groups is to encourage trade between countries and to protect the interests of trading group members. Free trade uses the raw materials from LEDCs. LEDCs often export them at low prices. This has led to multinational companies moving into developing countries to take advantage of low costs. This has been at the expense of small local businesses and damage to the environment.

To save the people in LEDCs from exploitation, **fair trade** agreements have been introduced. These agreements aim to benefit trade and investment in the countries by improving the working conditions and pay of local people. It is hoped that social and economic development will reduce the cost of operating businesses and increase the amount of profit given to workers. This should encourage reinvestment into future programmes.

did you know?

The EU is one of the world's largest trading groups.

Action Point Ⓐ

Name one retail outlet that sells fair trade goods.

Multinational companies

A **multinational company** is a company that operates in more than one country. A domestic company has no operation abroad. Multinational companies are responsible for two-thirds of world trade and are very influential in the world's economy. These companies are operated by a small number of people and are firm upholders of the principle of free trade. The largest multinational companies match, or exceed, the size and scale of some nations in wealth, power and trading; for example, the Gross Domestic Product (GDP is the total value of goods produced by a country or a company in a year) of General Motors was $164 billion in 1997, while the GDP for Norway was $153 billion in the same year.

Multinational companies have grown by creating products that sell well and by merging with other companies that produce similar services and products. Profits from the products are reinvested in the company to produce new consumer goods. The development of global communication technology has been a factor in the growth of multinational companies and has helped them to move their operations into various countries across the world while they are managed from the companies' headquarters in another country. Multinationals seek to make a large profit. This is done by moving to a location with an appropriate transport network, cheap ground rents and cheap labour. Such locations are usually based in developing countries.

> **did you know?**
>
> Multi-national companies are also known as transnational companies.

The impact of multinational companies

Multinationals have great economic power in a growing global economy. They have the power to move production from one country to another. The corresponding loss of jobs and income can have dramatic effects on local communities but multinational companies do not need to be loyal to any area of operation. Multinational companies are public companies that answer for their actions to the shareholders of the company. Shares in multinational companies are owned by individuals, institutions and pension funds. Most people have invested to make money so they are looking at profit rather than the ethics of a company's operation.

Aid

Aid programmes are the transfer of money, goods, services and expertise from one country (the donor) to another (the recipient).

- **Bilateral aid** is usually given by one country to another country in the form of a low-interest loan for a specific project. Bilateral aid is given by the UK and other countries to their former colonies.
- **Multilateral aid** is the money given by governments to international agencies. The agencies decide how the money will be spent. Many of the agencies that receive multilateral aid work for the UN.

- **Voluntary aid** is given by NGOs. These organizations are mainly charities such as Oxfam, Christian Aid, Save the Children, International Red Cross and Cafod. Most of the charities are based in industrial countries and raise money through public appeals, regular voluntary donations, mail order and charity shops. Their aid is more closely targeted to local needs and is usually very effective because they can plan aid delivery.
- **Relief aid** is a short-term measure which deals with emergency situations. It is usually given in response to a natural disaster such as flood, earthquake or drought or as an international response to war. Food, medical, health, water purification equipment, clothing, shelter and blankets are supplied to give relief.
- **Development aid** is given as a long-term solution to help a country's level of development by improving the quality of life of its people. Measures include health care, providing running water, practical help for farmers, community projects and initiatives.

Televised national events like Red Nose Day, Children in Need, the London Marathon and the Great North Run raise voluntary public donations for a wide range of charitable causes in the UK and abroad. Some events like Band Aid, organized by Bob Geldof and Midge Ure, are held to raise money for specific international problems, such as famine in Ethiopia. Sports Aid had a more general aim of helping the development of sporting activities in the UK and other countries, and Bill Clinton and Nelson Mandela are working to raise funds to help the South African AIDS Appeal.

UN aid agencies

Aid is a major aspect of the work undertaken by the UN. The UN's work is usually supported by NGOs. The following are examples of UN agencies.

- The World Health Organization (WHO) aims to improve the health of the world's people and to eliminate diseases that attack the developing world. It deals with the UN's response to world disease such as AIDS.
- The UN Development Programme (UNDP) aims to support countries achieve sustainable development. The UNDP may fund a project in a developing country to improve its system of education, transport, communication and health care.
- The World Food Programme provides food aid. Its aim is to eliminate world hunger. It supplies emergency relief aid in times of natural disaster. The UN Fund for Population Activities gives support with education and training for activities leading to family planning and population control. Unlike other UN funds, this fund operates on voluntary contributions from member states.

Sustainable development

Sustainable development can be defined as 'development which meets the needs of today without compromising the needs of the future'. It means that we should treat the world in such a way that we ensure a good quality of life for people now and in the future – that we create something that is sustainable. We need to accept and understand that the world does not have infinite resources. Once we have used up the resources, there will be no more. Action is needed on a global scale to protect the environment, the atmosphere and natural resources. Global action will be needed to find some alternative, renewable sources of energy.

Agenda 21

In 1992, the United Nations held an Earth Summit in Rio de Janeiro. The summit agreed to tackle the main threats to human existence – poverty, hunger and environmental destruction. The most significant of the agreements to come from this summit was Agenda 21. Agenda 21 is an action plan for moving towards sustainable development for the twenty-first century. It is based on the slogan 'Think globally, act locally' and aims to make all development socially, economically and environmentally sustainable. Everyone is expected to contribute to the objectives of Agenda 21. The agenda has been adopted by 178 governments.

In the UK, local authorities have prepared Agenda 21 policies for their area. Some people think that the proposals were over ambitious and cannot be implemented. Some authorities have moved a long way towards their Agenda 21 statements but in other authorities there is little sign that any improvements have been made.

Towards the future

The third UN conference was on climatic change and took place in Kyoto, Japan in 1997. It was attended by 160 nations. This conference required countries to reduce carbon emissions. It encouraged energy conservation measures, such as stricter standards for cars and electrical appliances, and environmentally friendly exercises such as recycling. The USA does not accept the outcomes of this conference, which are known as the Kyoto Protocol.

To achieve sustainable development will require individuals, communities and industry to accept the challenge and to change their current practices. The earth's resources will soon run out. We must:
- learn not to pollute the air, water and soil
- create less waste
- find environmentally friendly ways of disposing of waste
- stop harming the environment
- create and use alternative forms of energy (solar, wind, etc).

Only by consistent, concerted action will we be able to protect the environment.

Action Point

Name five Agenda 21 issues.

Action Point

Name three things that local authorities were expected to do to meet the objectives of Agenda 21.

Try these short questions

Questions like the ones below will appear in Section A of the exam paper. They require short, factual answers and are worth two marks for each question. Answers to these questions can be found on page 87.

1 What does 'WTO' stand for?
2 Name two developed countries.
3 What is a multinational company?
4 What does 'NGO' stand for?
5 Name two NGOs.
6 What is sustainable development?
7 Where and when was the first Earth Summit?
8 What is the slogan associated with Local Agenda 21?

Action Point (A)

Test yourself by answering the questions and then looking up the answers. Be honest with yourself – find out what you know and what you still need to learn!

Checklist for revision

	Know and understand	Need more revision	Do not know
I know what global inequality is	☐	☐	☐
I know what LEDCs and MEDCs are	☐	☐	☐
I know what the World Trade Organization is and what it does	☐	☐	☐
I know what free trade and fair trade agreements are	☐	☐	☐
I know what a multinational company is	☐	☐	☐
I understand the impact of multinational companies	☐	☐	☐
I know what aid is and how it is used	☐	☐	☐
I know what sustainable development is	☐	☐	☐
I know how Agenda 21 aims to help the future	☐	☐	☐

exam watch

How many did you get right? Some people find **COLOUR-CODING** their notes helpful.

9 Exploring global issues – the human and environmental problems

What you need to know

- How to question a basic argument and form your own opinions
- What poverty is and what it does
- How the world's finance is organized
- What human rights are and how they are abused
- What the arms trade is and what arms are used
- How global warming affects the planet
- What acid rain is and its effects on the earth
- How deforestation affects the world's ecosystems
- What an ecosystem is
- What you can do as a future citizen

Forming your own opinion

This chapter covers many of the issues facing the world today. There are many others. Some of these are listed at the end of the chapter. Remember that as a citizen you have rights, but these rights often require you to exercise responsibility for your own and other people's actions. You have the right to your own opinion, but you should make sure that your opinion is based on factual evidence. You should be able to outline your opinion clearly without being offensive to others. This is acting responsibly. Table 1 lists the elements that Oxfam thinks will be required by a global citizen.

Knowledge and understanding	<ul><li>Social justice and equality</li><li>Diversity</li><li>Globalization and interdependence</li><li>Sustainable development</li><li>Peace and conflict</li></ul>
Skills	<ul><li>Critical thinking</li><li>Ability to argue effectively</li><li>Ability to challenge injustice and inequalities</li><li>Respect for people and things</li><li>Co-operation and conflict resolution</li></ul>
Values and attitudes	<ul><li>Sense of identity and self-esteem</li><li>Empathy</li><li>Commitment to social justice and equality</li><li>Value and respect for diversity</li><li>Concern for the environment and commitment to sustainable development</li><li>Belief that people can make a difference</li></ul>

Table 1 The key elements of responsible global citizenship. *Oxfam.*

Poverty

Statement 25 of the UN Universal Declaration of Human Rights says that everyone has the right to 'a standard of living adequate for the health and well-being of themselves and their family, including food, housing, clothing and medical care'. People living in **poverty** do not have the means to provide these basic needs for themselves and their families. Poverty denies people of a basic **human right**. Poverty is a major cause of disease and illness, poor educational opportunity, unnecessary migration and despair.

A country's wealth is measured by how many goods it produces – its Gross National Product (GNP).

$$\text{Annual GNP per head} = \frac{\text{Total value of goods and services in US \$}}{\text{The country's population}}$$

Some people think that GNP is not a good indicator because the developing countries do not have accurate information about population, and the subsistence farming, on which many communities depend, is not included in the calculation. However, we do know that there is an unequal distribution of wealth throughout the world. Very few people in the developed world live in absolute poverty, whilst many people in the developing world are dying of hunger or struggling every day for survival.

Finance

The World Bank controls the money loaned to countries. It is the main organization to lend money to finance projects in developing countries. The IMF is responsible for managing the world economy by creating stability in trade between countries. To achieve this, the IMF places conditions or restrictions on the money loaned and as the IMF bases its operation on the free trade system, the powerful Western nations benefit from its operation. The World Bank loans a sum of money to a country. The country pays the loan, plus interest, back to the bank over a set period of time. The longer it takes to pay, the more the country has to pay back and the longer it will be in debt. In the 1970s, when large profits were made from the oil industry, the banks had lots of money and they loaned it to Latin America, Africa and Asia. Many countries have found it difficult to repay these loans. As a result, some African countries have fallen deeper into debt and now pay more in debt repayment than they spend on education and health combined. Many people believe that the Western world should do more to write off debts.

Human rights abuses

The United Nations Universal Declaration of Human Rights was signed in 1948. It states that:

> 'all human beings are born free and equal in dignity and rights. They are endowed with reason and conscience and should act towards one another in a spirit of brotherhood'.

The UN Commission on Human Rights supervises how the declaration operates. It monitors countries for human rights abuses relating to torture, imprisonment, the death penalty, and sexual and racial discrimination. The UN is helped in this monitoring by NGOs like Amnesty International (AI) and Action by Christians against Torture (ACT). In some countries people lose their freedom, and even their lives, because they think differently to a government and speak against its policies.

Human rights are abused in many areas of life when people are:
- not allowed freedom of expression e.g. to practise their religion
- tortured
- not granted a fair trial
- discriminated against
- not granted asylum from persecution.

Children are the most vulnerable group in any society. The UN Declaration of the Rights of the Child (1989) tries to stop children being abused or exploited. It sets out the rights of the child with respect to:
- **survival** – children have the right to a decent standard of living
- **development** – children have the right to education

Key ideas

To borrow money from the World Bank, a country must be a member of the International Monetary Fund (IMF).

did you know?

Jubilee 2000 is an organization that aims to eradicate Third World debts. Bono, of the pop group U2, has worked with this organization.

- **protection** – children have the right to be free from slavery, exploitation and cruelty
- **participation** – children have the right to express an opinion on decisions concerning them.

The issues of arms and weapons

The world spends more on arms than anything else. The arms trade is the manufacture and sale of a wide variety of military weapons, vehicles and equipment. It includes items such as fighter aircraft, tanks, missiles, guns and grenades.

Nuclear weapons were used for the first time in 1945 when the USA and Allied forces dropped bombs on the cities of Hiroshima and Nagasaki in Japan. At this time, only the USA had nuclear capability. Since then there has been a huge increase in the number of countries possessing nuclear technology because it is now cheaper to produce and also because countries want to protect themselves. One much-used weapon is the **landmine**. It is designed to be hidden under, on or near the ground and to explode when a weight is placed on it. The weight is usually a person or a vehicle. The Ottawa Treaty (1999) banned the use of landmines. The treaty was signed by 89 countries but the USA refused to sign.

Biological weapons include the use of viruses and bacteria which cause death in humans. **Chemical weapons** include toxic substances which will kill or disable people or poison food or water supplies. Biological and chemical weapons are capable of killing large numbers of people.

Global warming

Global warming is said to cause climate change by changing the world's temperature. The temperature has changed naturally over a period of time, but what is worrying scientists today is the speed at which these changes are now taking place because of human factors. As a result, droughts, floods and hurricanes have affected places that are not used to such extreme weather conditions. Ice sheets are starting to melt and sea levels are starting to rise.

Global warming is caused by:
- carbon dioxide (CO_2) trapping the heat reflected from the earth
- solar heat warming the land and sea
- CFCs from aerosols and refrigeration plants
- CO_2 from burning forests and rotting trees
- waste from humans and animals causing methane
- adding carbon to the atmosphere by burning fossil fuels
- oil and petrol emissions
- the use of nitrogen-based fertilizers.

did you know?

Developing countries spend more on arms than they spend on education. In the main, developed countries sell arms and developing countries buy them.

did you know?

Over 10 000 people are killed each year by landmines while 16 000 are injured or maimed.

Action Point

Name three human factors that contribute towards global warming.

When there is too much carbon in the atmosphere the heat from the earth's surface is trapped. This is known as the **greenhouse effect**. Greenhouse gases such as methane, water vapour, chlorofluorocarbons (CFCs) and nitrogen oxides trap the heat from the sun in the atmosphere. This causes climatic changes. An increase in gases causes a hole in the ozone layer, which exposes the earth to more radiation from the sun. This causes global warming.

Environmentalists argue that we need to reduce the amount of energy we use to slow down the rate of global warming. We should make our homes and industry more energy efficient and recycle used materials. Friends of the Earth and Greenpeace urge us to develop renewable energy sources, such as solar panels and wind turbines, and to reduce the use of fossil fuels, such as coal, oil and gas.

Acid rain

Rain is always slightly acidic because carbon dioxide is dissolved as the drops of rain fall through the atmosphere. Burning coal, gas and oil releases sulphur dioxide and nitrogen oxides into the atmosphere. When these dissolve into water droplets, they pollute the water cycle. The result is **acid rain**. Acid rain damages and can destroy trees. Acid rain can cause erosion to rock formations and can damage buildings, statues and bridges. Limestone buildings are particularly at risk. Acid rain can affect people's health because dry deposits can cause coughs and headaches. If water supplies are contaminated, then toxic chemicals from rain can be stored in fruit, vegetables and animals, contaminating the food chain. Other problems include the pollution of lakes and ponds. This will result in the loss of fish, birds, otters and other animals from the lakes. The environmental problems caused are more severe in Europe and North America.

did you know?
Pollution caused in Britain can travel across the sea to countries like Norway.

Acid rain can be reduced, but for an agreement to be effective all countries in the world will have to abide by it. Any agreement will be costly to implement. Acid rain can be reduced by:

- decreasing the emissions of sulphur dioxide from power stations
- decreasing emissions from cars
- using alternative energy sources
- having an international agreement
- raising public awareness and changing social habits.

Deforestation

Deforestation is caused by:

- slash-and-burn farming
- indiscriminate felling by logging companies to reach commercially useful types of trees
- clearing land to enlarge cattle ranches
- cutting down rainforest for industrial development and transport networks.

did you know?
Rainforests contain 50% of all the world's living species.

Section B questions

Section B will start with a piece of information – a source – that will be used to base the questions on. There is no choice – you must answer all the questions in this section.

Example 1

The following source and questions relate to Topics 1 and 2. The type of answers expected are shown after the questions. In the exam the questions will be in a booklet with space for your answers after each part of each question.

Section B

Answer **all** parts of the question in this Section.

Source A

Voting systems

Many people argue that the present system of electing a national government in Britain does not represent how people vote in elections.

The following chart shows the results of the General Elections in 1992 and 1997, using the system of first past the post.

Political Party	% vote 1992	Number seats won 1992	% vote 1997	Number seats won 1997
Conservative	43	336	31	165
Labour	35	271	44	418
Liberal Democrats	18	20	17	46

After the 1997 General Election the government set up a commission to look at electoral reform. The Jenkins Commission Report of October 1998 recommended that a system called AV plus should be introduced. This is the Alternative Vote System with a top-up element.

Exam type questions

a) With reference to Source A explain what voting system we use in General Elections in UK parliament. (5 marks)

b) Using Source A and your own knowledge outline the problems the 'first past the post system' can cause. (10 marks)

c) Using Source A and your own knowledge what was the recommendation of the Jenkins Commission? Give your own opinion of this voting system. (15 marks)

exam watch

Before you begin to answer the questions, read the text again, look carefully at the chart – what information is it telling you – who won the elections – why might one party in particular feel that the number of seats they won was not a true representation of the percentage (%) of the vote they gained? Read each part of the question thoroughly before you begin to answer it.

Marking your answers

For all examinations the people who mark the papers, the examiners, must follow the mark scheme. The questions in Section B will always have a levelled mark scheme. The answers in the mark scheme for this question would be something like this:

a) **Level 1 for 1–3 marks**
Name the first past the post system + one or two comments indicating that the person with the most votes wins.

Level 2 for 4–5 marks
Name the first past the post system + give a good description of how the system works.

b) **Level 1 for 1–3 marks**
A limited answer giving one or two of the problems.

Level 2 for 4–7 marks
A response which uses the source and makes some comments about unfair number of seats won for the percentage of the vote gained, under-representation.

Level 3 for 8–10 marks
A well-written response which makes full use of the information to draw conclusions.

You are expected to make comparisons between the two elections and proportion of votes cast for the parties. For example:

- In 1992 the Conservatives gained 43% of the vote and 336 seats and formed the government.
- In 1992 the Liberal Democrats gained 18% of the vote but only 20 seats, this was not a representative proportion of seats for the number of votes gained.
- In 1997 Labour gained 44% of the vote and 418 seats and formed the government – this was only 1% more of the vote than the Conservatives achieved in 1992 but Labour won 82 more seats.
- In 1997 the Liberal Democrats won 17% of the vote, 1% less than in 1992, yet gained 26 more seats in this election.

Conclusions to draw:

- The winning party and the one that forms the government has more votes cast against it than for it in each election.
- The number of seats won by each party does not reflect the percentage of votes cast for them.
- It is not a real representative system.

Marking your answers

The answers in the mark scheme for this question would be something like this:

a) **Level 1 for 1–3 marks**
Name of gas + one way of reducing emissions OR two ways of reducing emissions.

Level 2 for 4–5 marks
Name of gas + three ways of reducing emissions.
Carbon dioxide is the gas mentioned and the three ways to reduce emissions in the text are: use tidal power; use wind power; use either to produce hydrogen to power vehicles.

b) **Level 1 for 1–3 marks**
Very limited answer giving one or two facts from the source.

Level 2 for 4–7 marks
A clear explanation of two or three points using mainly information from the source.

Level 3 for 8–10 marks
A full answer using the source material and some personal knowledge.
Facts that could be mentioned include:

- The Severn estuary is suitable because it has the highest tidal range in the world – water levels rise by 27 feet.
- Joint funding provided by Government and the Welsh Development Agency.
- Government is committed to reducing emissions of gases that cause global warming by 20 per cent by 2020.
- Tidal power generator costs slightly more to build than a wind turbine generator but costs about the same to run.
- Tidal power does not vary as wind power does.
- Carbon dioxide is a greenhouse gas which causes global warming – traditional methods of generating electricity produce a lot of these gases.
- Emissions from petrol- and diesel-powered vehicles also produce greenhouse gases, hydrogen powered vehicles don't, another way of reducing emissions.

c) **Level 1 for 1–3 marks**
Basic response using the source only. Probably no mention of LA 21 or Kyoto.

Level 2 for 4–6 marks
A partial account referring to Agenda 21 and the slogan – think global, act local – mention of government's commitment to reduce emissions linked to Agenda 21 and/or Kyoto.

Level 3 for 7–9 marks
A clear account of the aims of Agenda 21 and/or the Kyoto Protocol; links between Agenda 21 and reducing emissions of greenhouse gases and their effect; links with emission reduction and clean energy sources – wind, wave and tidal power; possible mention of objections to some of these – blot on the landscape/harm to marine life.

Level 4 for 10–12 marks
A good explanation of LA 21 and the Kyoto Protocol; links between LA21, Kyoto and reducing emissions of greenhouse gases and their effect; links with emission reduction and clean energy sources – wind, wave and tidal power; possible mention of objections to some of these – blot on the landscape/harm to marine life.

Level 5 for 13–15 marks

A good, clear explanation of the aims of Agenda 21 and Kyoto and how clean sources of power can reduce emissions of greenhouse gases; mention of wind, wave and tidal power, and alternative power sources for vehicles which would also reduce greenhouse gases; relevant examples included and mention of objections to some wind farms – blot on the landscape; tidal power generators possible danger to shipping and harmful to marine life.

Facts that should be mentioned especially for level 4 and 5 mark ranges:

- Agenda 21 was one of the most important agreements to come from the 1992 Earth Summit in Rio de Janeiro. It set out a plan for sustainable development in the twenty-first century – hence the 21. Agenda 21 gave rise to the slogan 'think global, act local', which means we can all help to sustain and improve the environment. Governments, regions, local councils, businesses and industry and individuals are all expected to play their part. Each local council has set its own targets for sustainable development.
- The Kyoto Protocol came from the third conference on climate change that took place in Kyoto, Japan at the end of 1997. It was attended by 160 countries. The conference set targets to reduce greenhouse emissions by 2012, the targets were different for MEDCs and LEDCs. MEDCs had to introduce ways of saving energy, introduce controls on emissions from cars and increase measures to protect the environment such as recycling more glass, paper and cans.
- The main stumbling block has been the USA as they did not sign up to all the aspects of the Rio Agenda 21 and did not accept the Kyoto Protocol.
- Facts taken from the source should be included, as well as any relevant examples about objections to wind farms, etc.
- Mention could be made of electric cars reducing carbon dioxide emissions, especially good if the electricity has been generated from wind or tidal power.

Section D questions

Section D of the exam paper is the only section where you have a choice of questions to answer. This section deals with the three themes which run throughout the course, which are:

- Theme 1 Rights and responsibilities
- Theme 2 Decision-making, power and authority
- Theme 3 Participation in citizenship activities.

There will be one question for each theme. You must answer ONE question only in this section. You can choose which ONE of the three questions YOU want to answer.

The questions can relate to any of the topic areas you have studied. Read all the questions carefully, including the bullet points which are there to help you structure your answer. You do not have to use the structure suggested in the question, you can use your own if you wish. In this section choose the question which you know most about to answer. You are expected to bring your own knowledge to this question, be able to give examples of situations, give your opinions based on the evidence you provide and draw conclusions wherever necessary.

Once you have decided which question you are going to answer, think carefully about the structure of the answer – use the bullet points given in the question to help you and add more of your own if you can. Write out a plan for the essay, so that if you do not complete it in the time, the examiner can at least see the areas you would have included in more detail. Do not spend more than 3–4 minutes on this, it is an outline plan only.

In answering the question in this section, bring together your knowledge from the different topic areas you have studied and use any information collected from the media and/or case studies you have read or written to show your knowledge and understanding of the issues involved. If you use something from a media source (newspapers or TV), quote the reference for it (say which newspaper or TV programme the information came from).

This section is worth **30 marks**, the same as the other three sections of the paper. It is marked according to the mark scheme, which will have different levels of marks.

On the following pages there are two questions related to each theme. One question will show you the expected types of response for each level in the mark scheme and the other question will have a model answer with the examiner's comments to show how the answer could have been improved.

Theme 1 – Rights and responsibilities

Question 1

'One person's rights are some else's responsibilities.' Discuss this statement.

Your answer could include:

- an explanation of the terms
- the difference between legal and moral rights and responsibilities
- some comparisons between the rights and responsibilities of people in different roles and in different cultures
- a conclusion, expressing your opinion based on what you have written – do you agree or disagree with the statement?

Answers

Level 1 for 1–5 marks
A very limited answer with one or two definitions of the terms and examples of rights and responsibilities of, for example, parents and children. No real conclusions drawn.

Level 2 for 6–10 marks
Again some definitions of the terms and examples of how one person's right can be another's responsibility; for example, a child has the right to education, parents have the right to choose which school their child goes to and the legal responsibility to make sure their child attends school. Some cultural differences may be mentioned. A brief comment to agree/disagree with statement.

Level 3 for 11–15 marks
A response which covers the main points, includes definitions and shows some understanding of the terms and concepts, some examples given of different roles and some indication of cultural variations given. The conclusion is mainly related to the written work.

Level 4 for 16–20 marks
The response is quite well structured and includes definitions and explanations to show some knowledge and understanding, with some examples of how rights and responsibilities inter-relate, and some mention of cultural variations. A conclusion is drawn related to the evidence presented.

Level 5 for 21–25 marks
A good well-structured response covering all the main points and showing a thorough knowledge and understanding of the terms and concepts. The essay contains examples of the different rights and responsibilities of people in the different roles they have in life – for example, child, parent, carer, employee, employer, consumer, elector – and also the responsibilities of institutions such as the judicial system, the government, the police and the media (some, not all, of these would be included). Some knowledge of cultural variations is expected and a reasoned conclusion is drawn, based on the work presented.

Level 6 for 26–30 marks
An excellent account that is well structured and shows a thorough knowledge and understanding of the terms and concepts. Good use of a wide range of examples to illustrate varying roles – for example, child, parent, carer, employee, employer, consumer, elector – and the responsibilities of institutions such as the judicial system, the government, the police and the media (some, not all, of these would be included). An awareness of cultural variations is shown. A justified conclusion is presented, based on the evidence provided.

Within the responses the following would be expected:

- Explanations/definitions of rights and responsibilities – a right is something we are all entitled to; a responsibility is something we are expected to do; a legal right or responsibility is what we can or must do according to the law of the land; a moral right or responsibility is what we can expect or are expected to do according to the values of the society we live in.
- For mark levels 5 and 6 some explanation of how different cultures have different values in their society, and therefore different responsibilities, would be expected.
- A good selection of examples of the rights and responsibilities of people in different roles in life, drawing out how one person's right can be another person's responsibility. Possible examples could be drawn from children, pupils, parents, teachers, employers and employees, consumers, electors, councillors, etc.

A conclusion will be clearly explained and based upon the evidence presented in the response.

Answers

A possible answer could be something like the one below.

Plan for answer

1   Definition and some examples.
2   The development gap to explain MEDCs and LEDCs.
3   Fair trade and free trade.
4   How a multinational works.
5   Conclusion.

EXAMINER'S COMMENTS

A reasonable plan, it includes the main elements suggested in the question. Mention could be made of the World Trade Organization and what it does. Sectors of industry could be mentioned and related to MEDCs and LEDCs. No mention of the candidate's own opinion, although this may be evident from the response or stated in the conclusion.

STUDENT'S ANSWER

Multinational companies and world trade

A multinational company is one that operates and trades in more than one country, usually in many different countries around the world. They are usually plcs and have shareholders and boards of directors. Some examples of such companies are Shell, Nissan, MacDonalds, Heinemann, Café Direct, Microsoft, Cadbury Schweppes, Calvin Klein, etc.

The development gap is the difference between the richer and poorer countries of the world. The richer countries have well-developed economies and are generally known as the More Economically Developed Countries (MEDCs). The poorer countries do not have as much trade and industry and usually supply raw materials to other countries or multinational companies, and are known as the Less Economically Developed Countries (LEDCs). The MEDCs, for example, North America and Western Europe, have seen many social, economic and technological changes over many years. The LEDCs are not industrialized, their economies are not as developed and living standards are not as good. The differences between LEDCs and MEDCs are referred to as the development gap.

There are problems with policies on world trade. Most of the world and all the multinational companies like to operate within free trade groups or associations. The UK belongs to one of the largest of these, the European Union or EU. The aim of these free trade groups is to encourage trade between particular countries and to protect the industries and interests of the member countries. Free trade uses raw materials bought at low cost from LEDCs. The LEDCs do not have the industry to manufacture products from their raw materials.

(Continued on page 79.)

Continued...

Fair trade is where the LEDCs do benefit from the raw materials they produce. Fair trade organizations try to stop poor working conditions and encourage development of manufactured goods through investment in these processing and packaging industries in the LEDCs. That way the LEDCs gain more economic benefits from the extra profits this brings; for example, Café Direct.

Multinational companies are very powerful in the world economy and some of these multinationals have more wealth than some of the smaller countries.

Some multinationals exploit some LEDCs by paying low wages to workers and polluting the environment, while others have increased production of crops, created more jobs, and brought new industry and modern technology to the country.

Multinationals have grown because they have created and developed products which sell really well and have become popular all over the world, such as Coca Cola and Pepsi. Other multinationals have grown by merging with other large companies or by buying up smaller companies in the same or a different country.

A multinational company will look for opportunities to make a large profit when they consider manufacturing in a new country or region of the world. The technology revolution has also helped multinational companies as global communication is now very fast and easy, making it quick for a multinational to communicate with each branch of the company wherever it may be.

There is a great deal of difference between living standards in the MEDCs and LEDCs. If there were more fair trade agreements and more of the multinational companies operated with consideration for their workers and the environment, created more jobs and invested in more processing industries in LEDCs rather than exploitation of people and land, then the development gap could be reduced. Some multinational companies do try to do this.

EXAMINER'S COMMENTS

Quite a good answer, showing an understanding of terminology and the differences between more and less economically developed countries, and the trading practices involved in free and fair trade. Some very good relevant examples of multinational companies are given showing knowledge of a range of manufacturing. A good understanding of how multinational companies operate is provided and the concluding paragraph shows the candidate's opinion based on the evidence provided.

Improvements that could be made:

- To gain even more marks primary and secondary sectors of industry could have been identified.
- More about multinational exploitation with specific examples could have been included.
- What a multinational company may look for when deciding on a suitable site for development of a manufacturing or processing/packaging industry; for example, Nissan in Sunderland.
- The World Trade Organization could have been mentioned, what it does and the protests outside some of the meetings against globalization.
- The term globalization could have been explained.

Theme 3 – Participation in citizenship activities

Question 1

Charities and other organizations hold major fund-raising events. Many of these are televised. Select one charity or organization and show how you could contribute to an event.

Your answer could include:
- some examples of charities and organizations and what they do
- a brief description of some televised events
- an explanation of the influence of the media on the event
- how you could contribute to a specific charitable event.

Answers

Level 1 for 1–5 marks
A very limited answer – giving an example of a televised event and brief details of how a personal contribution could be made.

Level 2 for 6–10 marks
Some details about charities and organizations and televised events, with one or two comments on the influence of the media, an outline of a possible personal contribution.

Level 3 for 11–15 marks
A clear statement about what a charity is, with examples to explain the variety of organizations. Some accurate details of televised events and some comments on how the media influences these events. Clear details of how a personal contribution could be made to an event.

Level 4 for 16–20 marks
The response is quite well structured, giving a definition of a charity, including a range of examples to show a range of different charitable organizations. Clear and accurate details of televised events with comments showing knowledge and understanding of media influences. Details of how a personal contribution could be made to an event.

Level 5 for 21–25 marks
A good, well-structured response that includes all the areas within the question. A good definition of a charity and a range of examples to show the many areas in which charitable organizations operate. Clear and accurate details of televised events with evaluative comments showing knowledge and understanding of media influences. Details of how a personal contribution could be made to an event.

Level 6 for 26–30 marks
An excellent, well-structured and logical response is given, showing knowledge and understanding of charitable organizations and what they do. A good range of examples included to illustrate the many areas in which charities operate. Accurate details of televised events with integrated evaluative comments on the influences of the media. Clear details of how a personal contribution could be made to an event.

Within the responses the following would be expected, especially in level 5 and 6 responses:
- Charities are usually voluntary organizations run by people who are not paid for their involvement in the organization. The charity may employ

some people to carry out certain administrative duties but the work of fund-raising is done by local groups who work voluntarily.

- Some examples should be given which show an awareness of local, national and international charities and who they help. For example, a local charity working to raise money for a new piece of equipment for the local hospital; Childline operates at national level, raising money to pay for phone lines so children and teenagers can ring and receive help and advice; the Red Cross, Save the Children and Oxfam work on an international level, helping people especially when disasters strike such as earthquakes and flooding.

- Knowledge of the well-known telethons, such as BBC Children in Need and Red Nose Day, with an explanation of how they work. The London Marathon and the Great North Run started as sporting events to encourage mass participation in sport and how the 'fun run' element became a money-raising event through sponsorship. How television influences these events and how well they are advertised in the media, with evaluative comments indicating what a strong and powerful tool television can be.

- Details of how a personal contribution could be made to a charitable event, naming the event and the charity, and how funds could be raised.

Question 2

Pressure groups are more effective than political parties. Do you agree?

Your answer could include:

- how a pressure group differs from a political party
- different types of pressure groups
- how pressure groups and political parties operate
- your own opinion – do you agree or disagree with the statement?

Answers

A possible plan could be something like the one below.

Plan for answers

1   Definitions of a pressure group and a political party.
2   How pressure groups are different from political parties.
3   Political parties, some major and minor parties, elections and gaining power – locally and nationally.
4   Pressure groups – local, national and international – focus groups – trade unions – examples.
5   Why people may be involved in a pressure group rather than a political party – single issue, strength of feeling, all political parties are the same.
6   Own views related to points 3, 4 and 5 and a final conclusion.

EXAMINER'S COMMENTS

A good plan which has included all the main points required. It demonstrates some knowledge and understanding of the terms and issues involved in the question as outlined in points 3, 4 and 5. Personal views may be expressed throughout the response and not limited to the last paragraph. The personal opinion stated should be a reasoned opinion based on the information/evidence written in the answer.

STUDENT'S ANSWER

Pressure groups and political parties

A political party is a collection of people who share the same political views. They are national parties and produce policies on a wide range of issues. They campaign, especially around election time, and hope to win power in local and national elections to run councils or form the government and make changes to our society and the way we live. They use the media for party political broadcasts, publish posters, election leaflets and adverts, and newspapers usually support one party or another. They can have a great influence on the public.

A pressure group is a collection of people who try to influence a particular issue or an area of government policy. There are different types of pressure groups — they may be charitable or voluntary organizations, focus groups, trade unions, employers' organizations or groups who organize global campaigns.

Pressure groups are usually well organized and use a range of the mass media to put their views across to the general public. They organize protest meetings and marches, and campaign and organize petitions for people to sign to make their views known. They advertise and send out information to people through the post to try to get new members and donations. A pressure group usually concentrates on a single issue; for example, Greenpeace — Save the Whale campaign.

Some pressure groups are active on an international scale. The one that has been in the headlines recently is the Stop the War campaign, with protests organized in many cities all over the world on the same day. The main slogans were 'Don't attack Iraq' and 'Not in my name'. The protests showed that there were huge numbers of people in many countries against the war, but the protests were not successful in preventing war.

There are different types of pressure groups such as local voluntary and charity groups who just work in a local community — for example, to raise funds for a new community centre — or focus groups where people join together to voice their opinion about one local issue — for example, a new road, a school closure or opencast mining. They will usually contact local councillors and their MP. The focus group will only carry on until the issue is sorted out.

Trade unions are another example of a pressure group. They are a union of people working in the same type of job; for example, one of the teachers' unions is the NUT,

(Continued on page 83.)

Continued...

National Union of Teachers, they represent the views of many teachers in all types of schools. Trade unions are different because they can ask their members to go on strike to try to get what they want. During the last few months the Fire Brigade Union, FBU, have called national strikes to try to increase fire fighters' income.

Political parties produce their policies from meetings and conferences and for general elections print all these policies in one document known as a manifesto. In the weeks before an election there is a lot of campaigning, and it is the main news item on TV and in the newspapers. Each party tries to persuade people to vote for them so they will win the biggest number of seats and be in power to form the government of the country.

The main political parties are the Conservative Party, the Labour Party and the Liberal Democrats. Examples of smaller parties are the Green Party and the National Front. In other parts of Britain there are also national parties – Plaid Cymru in Wales, the Scottish Nationalist in Scotland, and the Unionist parties Sinn Fein and the SDLP in Northern Ireland.

All political parties have different views on how best to run the country – for example, how education, hospitals and social services should be run – and on membership of the EU. People join political parties because they share the same views and want to help their party to win power.

Political parties have to produce policies on so many different issues, and individuals may agree with some but not others. It is often said that there isn't very much difference between the main parties now and many people do not feel that these parties offer a real choice in policy. I have read that there are twice as many people joining pressure groups as are joining political parties.

Many people join a charitable organization or pressure group because they want to work to help that group achieve its aims. They have very strong views and believe in the same thing, and they really want to get involved and do something. The single issues that are campaigned for are emotive issues that arouse strong convictions and support; for example, Amnesty International campaigns against injustice and torture.

I think that pressure groups and political parties both have their place. They both use many forms of the mass media to put their point of view across, but they are fighting for different things. The political parties have opinions on many different issues and want to win votes and govern the country to change systems and society, while pressure groups will campaign for one issue either in a local community, nationally or internationally.

EXAMINER'S COMMENTS

An excellent, well-structured and logical answer showing a thorough knowledge and understanding of political parties and pressure groups. This candidate clearly explains the terminology, and uses a range of relevant examples to illustrate points, showing an awareness of some local, national and international issues.

Improvements that could have been made:

■ There is a conclusion based on the evidence presented, but the candidate has not clearly answered the question posed by giving their own opinion on whether pressure groups are more effective than political parties.

SPECIAL NOTES

When a question asks for your opinion, make sure you give your opinion quite clearly, it should be based on what you have written about – the evidence provided. The last paragraph in this answer could be changed to do this. It is very easy to miss this point, as this will be your last question and you may run out of time.

Try to structure your answer and keep your eye on the time. If time is running out then do your best to include your main points – use a list of bullet points if time is really short and give your opinion on the issue if asked to do so.

Glossary

Acid rain Rain contaminated by chemicals from burning fuels

Advertising Techniques used to persuade consumers to buy goods

Agenda 21 Action plan for sustainable development agreed at Rio Summit (1992)

Aid programmes Transfer of money, goods and expertise from one country to another

Authority A form of power accepted as a legal right to rule

Budget Economic statement about taxation and spending targets

Civil law Relates to people's private rights, such as boundaries and marital breakdown

Commonwealth A group of nations, many of which were formerly British colonies

Community All the people who live or work in an area

Consumer Person buying goods or services

Contract of employment Written document containing terms and conditions of employment

Crime Any illegal or unlawful act against property or people

Criminal law Relates to crimes against people or property

Culture Shared language, behaviour, traditions and values of a society

Deforestation Felling trees to make wood and paper products

Development gap Divide between the two-thirds of the world's population who live in poverty and the other third who live in plenty

Devolution Transfer or delegation of power to regional level

Discrimination Treating people less favourably than others because of their gender, ethnicity, religion, culture or disability

Economy How goods, services and finances are provided and managed

Ecosystem Relationship between rocks, soils, vegetation, living organisms, water, atmosphere and climate

Equal opportunities Fair treatment without discrimination for everyone

Ethnic identity Particular culture of a group within society

European Convention on Human Rights (ECHR) Identifies citizens' human rights

European Union (EU) Group of 15 states trading labour, goods and services in single market

Fairtrade Trade organizations giving workers a reasonable price for their goods and labour

Finance Money raised for development through taxation or borrowing

Free trade Use of low-priced raw materials and labour to create profit for multinational companies and countries

Freedom of speech The idea that people should be able to air their opinions without punishment

Global warming Climate change caused by industrial and domestic gases which destroy the protective ozone layer and expose the Earth to increased heat

Government Democratically elected members of parliament who set taxes to pay for public services and make laws for everyone to live by

Health and safety at work Responsibilities of employers and employees to ensure safe working practices

Human rights Basic entitlements to liberty, justice, privacy, education and freedom

Industry Businesses involving raw materials/natural resources to manufacture products, or services

Law-making Parliamentary process for designing new laws

Local government System of councils responsible for looking after people, services and facilities in a country or urban area

Media Newspapers, books and magazines, radio, television and video, advertising, cinema and the Internet

Multinational company Any free-trade business operating in several countries to keep costs low and profits high

North Atlantic Treaty Organization (NATO) Alliance of 19 countries committed to each others' defence

Political party People sharing the same views who fight elections to form a government

Poverty Insufficient food, clothing, housing, water, sanitation and medical care

Power The ability to influence or to rule

Pressure group People who join together to influence or change government policy

Racism Treating people less favourably because they are from a different race

Religion System of values and beliefs

Responsibilities Duties towards oneself and others

Rights Freedoms to which one is entitled

School community A number of people working and learning together, sharing the same values and rules

Sustainable development Meeting the needs of the present without compromising the needs of the future

Taxation Money taken from citizens by the government to finance public services

Third World Countries with poor living standards, high birth and death rates, high infant mortality and low life expectancy

Trade Any system for buying and selling goods and services

Trade union Collection of workers who join together to promote their common interests

United Nations (UN) Organization set up after World War II to promote international peace, security and co-operation

Voluntary organizations Support groups who raise funds for and awareness of specific community issues or special groups

Voting Citizens' opportunity to decide who should govern them

World Trade Organization (WTO) Free trade organization regulating import and export of goods between countries

Index

acid rain 59
advertising 42–3
Agenda 21 23, 53
aid 51–2
arms 58
authority 2, 3

banks 12, 13–14
biodiversity 60
budgets 27, 27–8
businesses 10, 12–13, 51

change, bringing about 18–20
charities 19, 52
children 2, 30–2, 57–8
citizenship iv
    activities 70–1
    responsibilities 3, 55–6
civil law 37
climate change 53, 58–9
Commonwealth 44
communities, local 3–4, 15–16
conflicts 46–7
consumers 32
councils, local 4, 16, 23, 27, 36
courts 37–8
crime 34–5
criminal law 37, 37–8

deforestation 59–60
democracy 22–3, 25–7
developing countries *see* LEDCs
development, sustainable 53, 60
development gap 49–50
devolution 17
discrimination 4–6, 15, 33

economy 11–12, 27–8
    global 57
ecosystems 59–60
elections 16, 22–3, 25–6
electoral systems 17–18
employment 8–9, 33
energy 53, 58–9
environment 53, 58–60
equal opportunities 4–5
EU (European Union) 24–5, 28, 32, 33, 36, 38, 44
euro (single currency) 28
exam paper iv, v

fair trade 50
finance
    global 57
    local councils 16
    personal 13–14
financial services 12–13
focus groups 19, 20
free trade 50, 57
freedom of speech 40

GDP (Gross Domestic Product) 51
global citizenship 55–6
global warming 58–9
GNP (Gross National Product) 56
government 22, 23, 27–8
    devolution 17
    local 4, 16, 23, 27, 36
greenhouse effect 58, 60
Gross Domestic Product (GDP) 51
Gross National Product (GNP) 56

health and safety 9
human rights 1, 28, 40, 46, 56
    abuses 57–8

IMF (International Monetary Fund) 57
industry sectors 11, 12
inequality, global 49–50, 56
inflation 27
information technology 12, 17, 26, 40, 42
International Monetary Fund (IMF) 57
international relations 44–7
Internet 12, 17, 26, 40, 42

laws 30–2, 35–8
    see also discrimination; employment;
human rights
LEDCs (Less Economically Developed
Countries) 11, 49–50, 50, 51, 56
legal system 37–8
Less Economically Developed Countries
see LEDCs
lobbyists 19
local communities 3–4, 15–16
local councils 4, 16, 23, 27, 36
local economy 12

MEDCs (More Economically Developed
Countries) 11, 49, 56
media 40–3
More Economically Developed Countries
(MEDCs) 11, 49, 56
multinational companies 11, 50, 51

national economy 11–12, 27–8
NATO (North Atlantic Treaty
Organization) 46
new technology 12, 17, 26, 40, 42
newspapers 40, 41, 41–2
NGOs (non-governmental organizations)
46, 52, 57
North Atlantic Treaty Organization
(NATO) 46
Northern Ireland 47

opinions iv, 55
ownership
    businesses 10, 51
    media 41

parents 2, 30–2
parliament 23, 30, 36

personal finance 13–14
police 34–5
political parties 18, 19, 22, 22–3
poverty 56
power 2–3
pressure groups 19, 20
protests, peaceful 20

racism 5
rainforests 59–60
referenda 18, 26
resources 53, 59
responsibilities 2, 3, 55–6
revision hints v
rights 1–2, 42, 55
    see also discrimination; employment;
human rights

schools 2–3, 4
Section A v, 85–8
Section B v, 62–9
Section C v, 70–1
Section D v, 72–84
sectors of industry 11, 12
single currency (euro) 28
Social Chapter (EU) 33
sustainable development 53, 60
systems of government 22

taxation 13–14, 27, 27–8
television 40, 42, 43
themes iv
Third World countries *see* LEDCs
topics iv
trade 12, 50, 57
trade unions 19, 20

UK (United Kingdom)
    democratic system 22–3, 25–6
    economy 11–12
    and EU 24, 28, 44
    international relations 44, 46, 46–7
    media 41–2
    see also devolution; laws; local councils;
parliament
UN (United Nations) 44, 45–6, 52, 53
    Universal Declaration on Human
Rights (1948) 40, 46, 56, 57–8
unions 19, 20
United Kingdom *see* UK
United Nations *see* UN
USA (United States of America) 53, 58

values 2, 15
voluntary organizations 19
voting 16, 17–18, 23, 25–6

weapons 58
work 8–9, 33
World Bank 57
WTO (World Trade Organization) 50